THE RAINBOW MANSIONS

by
JOHN HAWKINS

CON-PSY PUBLICATIONS MIDDLESEX

First Edition
2002

© John Hawkins

Published by

CON-PSY PUBLICATIONS
P.O. BOX 14,
GREENFORD,
MIDDLESEX, UB6 0UF.

ISBN 1 898680 28 0

CONTENTS

Chapter 1
"CLEARING THE MISTS OF TIME"

"The sum of generations is therefore: fourteen from Abraham to David; fourteen from David to the Babylonian deportation; and fourteen from the Babylonian deportation to Christ" **(Matthew 1:17)**

The Old Testament, the first part of the Christian Bible, is the collection of books comprising the sacred Scriptures of the Hebrews: the Pentateuch, the Historical Books, the Wisdom Books and the Prophets.

All these books contain the story of God's chosen people moving through time like a beam of light in search of a final resting place. Through slavery and plague, famine and war, it came to rest in sweet repose above a little town called Bethlehem. This beam of light became the light of the world for all generations to come - Jesus Christ.

Two thousand years have passed and Christians of all denominations have preached eternal life through hymns, prayers, sermons or through a system of religious doctrine, proclaimed by ecclesiastical authority as true.

The subject of eternal life is not a favourite topic for discussion with the clergy or church authorities, but stirs the lay-person. This is not a subject we should be afraid to explore, but a sweet fruit to be tasted and not a bitter herb. At the very mention of it, people are generally left suspended on the edge of their seats in an empty cloud of mist.

After Jesus was crucified on the cross he was buried in the tomb. He rose on the third day. Was this really the only evidence of eternal life that he gave us? I think not. The gospels are full of quotations and stories of Jesus, giving us an insight into eternal life.

Jesus was a man of mystery, because he was without sin; for a man who has sinned holds no mystery. Let us now clear the mist and I will give you the evidence that Jesus told us through the gospels. Gospel means good news, concerning Jesus, the son of God. I hope that you will be able to share in my joy as I begin with what is for me the most important quote from the Bible, giving so much

4

hope to mankind:

"In my Father's house are many mansions: if it were not so, I would have told you. I go to prepare a place for you." **(John 14:2)**

The Father's house is the heavenly realms, the many mansions being the different places within these heavenly realms. As we make our transition from earth to the heavenly realms, it is the way in which we have lived our life on earth that will determine our place within one of these mansions.

As we now begin to explore the evidence in the Old Testament, the reason for the choice of title for this book: *"The Rainbow Mansions"* will become clear.

After the great flood, in Genesis, God said to Noah,

"... This is the token of the covenant which I make between me and you and every living creature that is with you, for perpetual generations: I do set my bow in the cloud, and it shall be for a token of a covenant between me and the earth." **(Genesis 9:12)**

This was the very first covenant that God made with mankind. The colours of the rainbow play a most important role in our daily lives. Apart from the usual scientific explanation for the rainbow, there is a spiritual explanation. The rainbow is a recurring theme in the Bible, through the Old and New Testaments, from Genesis to the Book of Revelation. The rainbow consists of God's own seven colours and today the rainbow in the sky is still a reminder of God's judgement of man, when God flooded the earth. The most exciting part in connection with the rainbow is that these colours are seen around the physical body. The aura, nimbus or halo, is usually associated with the saints. Every human being, good or bad, emanates an aura of some kind. This aura, as individual as a fingerprint, is a spiritual self-judgement.

In the book of Exodus we have another judgement, by way of a breastplate, which God ordered to be made for the High Priest, Aaron, to wear when he entered the sanctuary, as a reminder to the people of the sins of the Jewish nation and that they were before God always. The breastplate was adorned with four rows of precious stones,

"... a sard, topaz and emerald for the first row, for the second row, a garnet, sapphire and diamond, for the third row, a

5

hyacinth, a ruby and an amethyst; and for the fourth row, a beryl, a cornelian and a jasper ..." **(Exodus 28:17-21)**

These stones when reflected through light would give off a kaleidoscope of colours. This breastplate was so important because each precious stone represented one of the twelve tribes of Israel. We will come back to these precious stones when we look at the top mansion of all, in the Book of Revelation.

Many people can see the spiritual aura around the physical body; each will see a different shade of the basic seven colours, according to their own gift. My own experience of seeing auras is that the dominant colour is yellow and into this gently blends any of the other six colours of the spectrum. The more spiritually developed a person is, i.e. the better their attitude towards their fellow man and nature, the brighter the yellow in the aura, with any one or two of the other colours inside the yellow, i.e. green, blue, indigo or violet. The aura of a person who is materialistic is still dominated by the yellow, with red and/or orange usually present, mingled with one of the other inside colours. The natural personality of a person is indicated by their aura; mood swings will alter the colouring. Those people with good spiritual auras are not necessarily those who attend church, confess their sins or partake in Communion. When a person tells a deliberate lie, the physical mind goes into turmoil and for whatever reason in the opposite direction from the truth. This causes a disturbance/vibration in the aura - the aura cannot lie. Our minds and personalities have both a physical and spiritual side, constantly in conflict, giving us the choice between good and evil.

Throughout the ages artists have painted saints and biblical characters with exaggerated auras, as if these are the only people with an aura. Stained glass windows in most churches also display auras around religious figures. Many great artists will have painted auras around the saints out of tradition and politeness, but somewhere along the line there must have been an artist with what I would call the eye of faith or sensitivity of the spirit to see spiritual auras, and with an understanding of its purpose would give a good measure of colour to do justice to the holy figures.

We are dual purpose beings; we are both physical and spiritual. God said,

6

"Let us make man in our image, after our likeness ..."
(Genesis 1:26)

The spiritual man is the part of us which will inherit eternal life: it is the physical man who will return to the dust. This is, of course, no great secret. St Paul, a hero of mine, has a reputation in Christian circles for being difficult to understand; he speaks a very simple language for me. He has no problem in telling us this. Here are a few of his many quotes:

"But some man will say, How are the dead raised up? and with what body do they come?" **(1 Corinthians 15:35)**

"It is sown a natural body; it is raised a spiritual body. There is a natural body, and there is a spiritual body." **(1 Corinthians 15:44)**

"Now this I say, brethren, that flesh and blood cannot inherit the kingdom of God; neither doth corruption inherit incorruption." **(1 Corinthians 15:50)**

As we are dual purpose beings, we now need to know how the physical is attached to the spiritual, and how, when the time comes, they separate.

We now turn to the Book of Ecclesiastes, Chapter 12. This is the only place in the Bible where the aura and the silver cord are mentioned. Here we have the most marvellous explanation of the ageing process leading to death; how each part of the body ceases to function up until the point of death and the separation of the spiritual body from the physical body. Verse 6 is the crucial verse - here we are given absolute proof of the existence of the aura and the silver cord. At the point of death the aura and the silver cord separate from the physical body and it is this spiritual body that returns to the many mansions. This has been the divine plan from the very beginning of God's creation; we have a physical and a spiritual body.

This chapter (Ecclesiastes:12) is written in symbolic language and each section deals with a different part of the body. Verse 5 tells us of man going to his long home, this long home being the many mansions of the heavenly realms - eternal life. Verse 6 opens, for me, the floodgates of delight - here we have manna from heaven!

"Or ever the silver cord be loosed, or the golden bowl be

broken, or the pitcher be broken at the fountain, or the wheel broken at the cistern." (**Ecclesiastes 12:6**)

The silver cord is a duplicate of the umbilical cord, which connects mother and child in the physical body. At the time of physical birth the umbilical cord severs or is cut, giving life for the first time. The silver cord is the spiritual cord which is attached to the physical body, both male and female. This cord, as with the aura, can only be seen through the eye of faith. The golden bowl is symbolic for the aura, which is more easily seen around the head. The aura looks like a golden bowl. At death this golden bowl appears to crack, break and to disintegrate. At the same time, when the cord is severing, because the aura is part of the spiritual body, the aura is pulled back into the cord, giving our spiritual body the record of our earthly life. We are, therefore, then drawn to our natural place within the many mansions. When the silver cord severs at death, the spiritual body is born - this is the second birth.

The pitcher and wheel mentioned in verse 6 represent the internal organs breaking down at death.

Verse 7 sums up the whole idea of eternal life:

"Then shall the dust return to the earth as it was: and the spirit shall return unto God who gave it." (**Ecclesiastes 12:7**)

In life, the silver cord enables the spiritual body to freely move about, when out of the physical body. The spiritual body is of a much higher vibration than the physical body and as such is able to pass through earthly matter, e.g. a wall, window or door. The cord does not get tangled around earthly matter, distance is no object; the cord remains attached to the physical body by a network of threads. The silver cord cannot be seen by the naked eye, but only through the eye of faith, and works through the sensitivity of the spirit. It is attached around the area of the solar plexus, which is the network of nerves within the stomach, and is itself like a cobweb of threads. As a young boy I learnt to feel its gentle tug and I became aware of its purpose. It can flow backwards and forwards and streams out from the spirit within, and is a direct prayer line to God. When used correctly, when in deep meditation, your prayers will flow out along this cord, causing an outpouring of the spirit and you will experience a gentle fluttering sensation. It is that same sensation felt when falling in love, or when someone close is ill. It will give a gentle tug if we bring to mind a loved one who lives far away. When we see a new born baby it flows out as if to greet the child personally, when we see a handicapped child it will flow out, leaving us feeling quite depleted. The spiritual body is the part of us that never grows old and when the cord severs, when this life is up, it returns on a journey familiar to itself, to the Creator.

We now turn to Jesus, who, through his famous conversation with Nicodemus, illustrates this point. Many take this piece from the Bible as the basis for their "born again" faith. It is in **St. John 3:1-13** that Jesus explains the two births and the relationship between the spirit and the physical body:

"There was a man of the Pharisees, named Nicodemus, a ruler of the Jews: The same came to Jesus by night and said unto him, 'Rabbi, we know that thou art a teacher come from God: for no man can do these miracles that thou doest, except God be with him.' Jesus answered and said unto him, Verily, verily, I say unto thee, Except a man be born again, he cannot see the kingdom of God. Nicodemus saith unto him, How can a man be born when he is old? can he enter the second time into his mother's womb, and be born? Jesus answered, Verily, verily, I say unto thee, Except a man be born of water and of the Spirit, he cannot enter into the kingdom of God. That which is born of the flesh is flesh, and that which is born of the Spirit is spirit. Marvel not that I said unto thee, Ye must be born again. The wind bloweth where it listeth, and thou hearest the sound thereof, but canst not tell whence it cometh, and whither it goeth: so is every one that is born of the Spirit. Nicodemus answered and said unto him, How can these things be? Jesus answered and said unto him, Art thou a master of Israel, and knowest not these things? Verily, verily, I say unto thee, we speak that we do know, and testify that we have seen; and ye receive not our witness. If I have told you earthly things and ye believe not, how shall ye believe, if I tell you of heavenly things?" **(St. John 3:1-13)**

Nicodemus was a very important man in Jewish society, a member of the Sanhedrin, which was the governing body of the Jewish council. He was a very learned man, steeped in the faith of the Torah, which is the first five books of the Old Testament, the basis of the Jewish faith. It must be noted that he visited Jesus by night, afraid to be seen with him.

Here we have Jesus explaining to Nicodemus that we all have two births. The first birth is into the physical world from our mother's womb, the second from the physical into the spirit world. He tells Nicodemus that no-one can see the kingdom of God unless they leave their earthly body and are reborn into the spirit world, or many mansions. Nicodemus fails to understand what Jesus is telling him; he is still thinking of his earthly birth. Jesus then raises the conversation to a higher spiritual level. He compares the wind with the spirit; the Hebrew word for spirit also means wind. Jesus tells Nicodemus that we can hear the wind and it blows where it pleases; where it comes from and where it is going, we do not know. We have no authority over the elements and so it is with the spirit. We do not know if the spirit enters at conception, during development or at birth. At one time a person was pronounced dead when the heart had stopped for a specified period of time; now a person is pronounced dead when the brain as well as the heart has ceased to function. A person is only truly dead when the spirit has left the body - but we do not know at which point this happens.

Nicodemus is even more confused and asks how all this is possible. Jesus answers, *"Art thou a master of Israel, and knowest not these things?"*. He cannot believe that Nicodemus does not understand. How was he, therefore, to get his message across, when a man such as Nicodemus could not grasp the idea of the dual purpose being, of a first (earthly) and second (heavenly) birth?

Jesus did not speak in parables, as was customary with the multitude, with Nicodemus, but used "verily", giving facts, the truth. This was the first time that we hear of Jesus opening up with the message of the dual purpose being.

Let us look now at **1 John 5**:

"This is he that came by water and blood, even Jesus Christ; not by water only, but by water and blood. And it is the Spirit that beareth witness, because the Spirit is truth." (**1 John 5:6**)

Here we learn that even Jesus had a normal human birth. Water and blood, amongst other things, make up the physical body, and as we have already talked about, the spirit holds the record of our earthly life. Verse 8 says:

"And there are three that bear witness in earth, the spirit and the water, and the blood; and these three agree in one." (**1 John 5:8**)

Here we have the proof of a physical and spiritual body, that the physical body is made up of the three elements mentioned here: blood, water and the spirit. Verse 9 says:

"If we receive the witness of men, the witness of God is greater: for this is the witness of God which he hath testified of his Son." (**1 John 5:9**)

God's final solution was to send Jesus Christ, as a physical man, to earth; a man, containing a spirit - the key to eternal life. He was sent to prove that there is eternal life.

When questioned by Pilate, Jesus replied:

"Mine is not a kingdom of this world. If my kingdom were of this world, my men would have fought to prevent my being surrendered to the Jews. As it is, my kingdom does not belong here." *Pilate said, 'So, then you are a king?'. Jesus answered, 'It is you who say that I am a king. I was born for this, I came into the world for this, to bear witness to the truth."* (**St John 18:36-38**)

Chapter 2
"MY OWN GIFTS"

My first childhood memories go right back to when I was still in nappies. Afternoon naps, after being fed and bottled, were something of a mystery to me. My mother would put me into my cot, in my parents' bedroom, and quietly walk out of the room. My father would be asleep in another room, after his night shift at the local factory. After about three or four minutes, I would be visited by several children. They would put their hands through the bars of the cot to touch me, and tug at my blankets. These children were always happy and smiling. As I recall there were four children: a half-caste girl and three white boys. They spoke to me, but I could not hear them. I could see them laughing and giggling and I understood their gestures in play. I can't remember sleeping, as I was supposed to. I thought that my mother put me into my cot so that these children could come and play with me. The children would disappear as my mother entered the room. I wondered why this happened. My older brothers and sisters did not disappear when my mother entered the room. As I got older, I realised that these children could come and go at will. In my early days at school, I would find it hard to concentrate as these children would be running about the classroom, in front of the blackboard. I received many a slap on the back of the head from a teacher for laughing out loud in class. I was so glad to see them; they knew that I could see them and I knew that they could see me. They seemed oblivious to everyone else and only played with me in the classroom and at home.

For many years these children were regular visitors; I took them for granted as they became part of my life. I never had names for them or gained any information about them as there was no communication in that way between us. I realised that they were different from human beings. It was the look in their eyes that gave it away. Their eyes would glow. They were so alive with colour, like shining ice. To look into their eyes was to give the whole being. I didn't need any other information. This has always been the case with spirits I have encountered. Once you have eye contact, they draw you in. These were the happiest children I have ever met. They were vibrant with life - so energetic. There was no fear on either side. There was nothing to suggest that these children were suffering or had suffered in any way; they were neither undernourished nor deformed. I often wondered what had caused their passing as they gave no indication.

Their dress did not seem very different from mine, growing up in the fifties. They were not in rags or in shoddy clothes; they wore socks and boots and coats with wide lapels. They were probably from the generation of my older brothers and sisters, born around the thirties. They were not all from the same family, probably from the same area. Their ages ranged from about five years to ten years old. There was a boy of about five, a girl of about seven and the two older boys, who looked similar and so were probably brothers, were about nine and ten years old. The little girl was beautiful, and being a half-caste, a rarity for me at that time. My personal view is that they were probably children who passed over during the Second World War.

From the age of about ten I entered a new phase and my spirit playmates became a wonderful memory. I had gained the knowledge that there was no fear or sadness in death, even for young children.

I was growing up in a household which had to be quiet because my father worked a night shift and slept during the day. We all had to creep around the house and whisper in conversation. I had to shut the door quietly, make myself a snack without making a noise and build the fire in the hope that no coal or wood would fall and wake my father. I was not allowed to fly the pigeons or bring my bike up to the house until he was awake. I had one real friend, Henry, who was slightly older than I and lived just a few doors away. When Henry was busy, my mother at work and father asleep, I was alone in the house. I started to have out-of-body experiences. The first time that this happened was on a really hot day. I went for a lie down on the settee. I thought that I was falling to sleep; the next thing I knew, I was floating up and was soon able to look down at myself on the settee. Something else had opened up and this became the best game I had ever had.

At this time, at the age of ten, I did not understand what was

13

happening to me. Each time it happened I did not know if I had just fallen asleep and had a dream or fallen into a semiconscious state. It was a very comfortable feeling. I would become aware of a "filling-up" sensation, from my feet to my head and a warm, fluttering sensation in my stomach. My breathing would slow right down. As my spirit body rose up towards the ceiling I was no longer aware of any feeling in my physical body; all feeling was transferred to my spirit body. My thoughts would control my movement - so that I did not collide with the ceiling or the walls - like autosuggestion. The spirit world is a world of thought, where most things are achieved by thought alone. As I came out of the body, I would be facing the ceiling and would then make a natural turn so that I was looking back down to earth, at myself. This would happen as I had risen about two feet away from my body. Once up, I would feel naked and realise that I had a duplicate. I could see two of me, the physical body left resting on the settee and the spirit body glowing all around me. I learnt to move in all directions, once out of the body, by mere suggestion. As a child I learnt that by putting myself in a relaxed state I could bring on one of these experiences. It was always as a result of some disturbance, however, that I would be jolted back into my physical body, and I could never figure out how I had got down so quickly.

Around the walls in the sitting room there was a picture rail, about eighteen inches from the ceiling. As I floated around the room, I could see chips in the top of this picture rail and splashes of paint colour from previous years. From the floor these marks were not visible. To test myself I would climb up the stepladder and could verify that these marks were indeed real.

As a teenager I developed a yearning to take this a step further and to venture outside of the house. I was very afraid at first - in case I floated away! I soon realised that I was able to pass through matter, in my spirit body, and leaving my physical body in the house would pass through a window to the outside world. Once outside I travelled much closer to the ground than inside; I could walk along the floor and even fly along near to the ground if I wanted to travel more quickly. I was always attached to my physical body by what looked like a beautiful silvery-blue pyjama cord. This cord seemed to be streaming out from the back of my head on my physical body,

14

attached to my spirit body at the bottom of my back. It would never get tangled and would stretch as far as I wanted to go, like a piece of elastic! It took only a few minutes for me to get myself into the required relaxed state, once I had mastered the technique, to bring on an out-of-body experience, and each experience seemed to last longer than it actually did - only about five or six minutes. I loved these experiences - I became as free as a bird, I came to know the feeling of floating, flying effortlessly and surging along at speed. I remember only one bad experience, when I was in my late teens; I was out of the body (in the house), when I became "physically" aware of a loud noise. I shot back into the body so quickly that it made me ill. I remember seeing my physical body jolt; I had never seen that before or seen it since. I had started to regain consciousness before my spirit body had re-entered my physical body. A person is first and foremost a physical being and secondly a spiritual being. I learnt by trance/meditation to attain the level of relaxation required to bring up my spiritual consciousness and lower my physical consciousness, to have an out-of-body experience. In this case the physical body reacted first before the spirit body had the chance to return, creating disharmony between the two. Before this I had never been aware of the reason for the spirit body's return. After this I suffered stomach pains for many months.

During the summer holidays, before I started at secondary school, I had a completely new experience. I was sitting on the kerb-side outside of my house when a neighbour's dog ran yapping up the garden path and straight under the wheels of a passing car. The driver stopped the car and got out. The dog seemed to be panting heavily. I stood and watched and saw what looked like smoke coming from the dog's mouth or head, rising above the animal. I thought that it looked like my breath on a winter's day - but this was mid-August and a very hot day! Eventually the smoke wavered and took on the exact shape of the dog. I was amazed as I watched it disappear into thin air. While I was transfixed to this sight, the dog's owner had come out with a blanket. The driver of the car was most apologetic and offered to take the dog to the vet. Quick as a flash I said, "Oh, it's alright, he has gone to heaven!". The assembled group then realised that the dog was dead. I had witnessed, for the first time, a spirit body leaving a physical body at the point of death. I was, over the years, to witness this many times with animals, giving me proof of an animal kingdom within the many mansions.

One of my great passions in life has been pigeons. As a boy I would spend hours in the garden with my pigeons, watching them, feeding them, listening to them and dreaming of the day when I would be old enough to race them. As I sat on the garden bench one afternoon studying the pigeons, I had such a strange feeling. I was aware of something happening around me. I felt damp and warm and slightly claustrophobic. I sensed a slight pressure over my whole body; I had the feeling of being enveloped in a thick layer of cottonwool. It was not an uncomfortable feeling by any means. At my left side a figure very gradually came into focus, becoming brighter and brighter. It was a tiny, white-haired old lady. I was not frightened at all. She looked at me and smiled, her eyes were shining and a beautiful bright blue in colour. Her resemblance to my mother was overwhelming. She spoke to me and said, "You don't know who I am, do you? I am your grandmother, Mary-Anne. You are little John, the youngest, and Joan is the oldest.". I did not reply but remember feeling that it was obvious that she was something to do with my mother. I kept looking over my shoulder to my mother, who was working in the kitchen. I could see her at the kitchen window, and wondered if she could see my visitor. I had never met my grandmother in life, she passed away before I was born, and had no photographs of her. She sat with me for only a minute and then just faded away. This was my first encounter with an adult spirit and the only relative I have ever seen in the spirit. I later spoke with my sister, Joan, and she confirmed that my grandmother had indeed been named Mary-Anne.

As I look back over the years, as I write this book, I realise what a gentle introduction I was given to each of my gifts and that they unfolded, one after another, in a logical sequence. They were mystical, mysterious and unexplained and I believe there to be a higher authority controlling this situation, making sure that I was never frightened or upset. I had no control over any of this. It is only now, because of my knowledge of the Bible, that I feel able to talk about these gifts and to offer some explanation.

As a teenager I started to visit the cinema with my friend, Henry. On one occasion as I sat in the darkness, relaxing into the film, I became aware of a faint pale light around people's heads. The light became brighter and brighter. I would try to watch the film but in the end was prevented from doing so. The lights became an irritation and I had to question what they were. Each person had a half to a one inch band of light around the head. As these built up I had to disregard the film; I was more drawn to the lights around people's heads than the film. I had begun to see auras.

From this day I started to see auras on a regular basis. As this gift developed, I realised that this band of light contained colours - the colours of the rainbow. For me, everybody has this band of light around their head; when I meet someone, the light is part of that person - I never see a person without seeing an aura. Over time I learned to look at people in a certain way and to draw out the colours of the aura. I can do this, in a certain atmosphere, when I stand back, relaxed and not preoccupied with anything else; I can request this information for myself, from myself. I realised that there was a link between the colours and personality types. At first I would study relatives and friends - it was easier with people I knew. These were the very people, however, with whom I could not share my gifts. My parents, family and friends were simple working people, too busy to notice me - I did not dare to tell them what was happening to me, I knew that no-one would understand. I had come to realise that I was quite unique and that there was no-one else in my immediate circle with these gifts. I was a shy, sensitive young man and this new way of life became, at times, a source of great embarrassment to me, as I was able, in reading auras, to pick up people's thoughts. I remember thinking that I could do without this "gift" and questioned its purpose. However, it was all very fascinating to me as I began to live in two worlds; and I now accept that all this is part of who I am. To this day, I am still discovering how amazing this aura is, and how it works.

I left school at the age of 14 and decided to learn the art of judo. I was a devoted student and, in time, graded at Black Belt 2nd Dan (Instructor) level. This helped me to overcome my shyness. I had always been a boy whose feelings were easily hurt and I blushed

17

very easily. My personality, combined with my new-found ability to read auras, sometimes made life very awkward for me. I could, through no fault of my own, pick up someone's feelings and do what I thought was a bit of mind-reading.

One evening I was training a group of police cadets at the judo club. It was a very strenuous and physical session. I distinctly remember feeling absolutely drained and after leaving the club, treated myself to a meal at my favourite restaurant. After enjoying a lovely meal, I started the twenty minute walk home. This was a real struggle - I was very tired and full of food. As I walked along in the darkness I sensed someone following me. I soon became aware of something around my person - not at the back or at the side or at the front, but more like a closeness. I began to feel a surge of unbelievable energy; I felt like I was a vase filling up with water, like I was eight feet tall. I was quite bewildered, feeling overshadowed and enveloped in a cobweb of cottonwool. However, this was not an unpleasant sensation. To this day, I have no recollection of the rest of my journey home: I was somehow jolted back to reality on reaching my front door.

When I got into the house I still felt full of food and even more drained than earlier. I wondered if I had food poisoning or if I had just overstretched myself at the judo club. My mother was watching the television and when she turned to look at me, saw no difference in my wellbeing. I expected for her to notice a physical change in me - but I had no reaction from her. So I said 'goodnight' and called it a day.

As I sat on the side of my bed, the strange feelings and sensation began to well up inside of me once more. I tried again to account for these feelings - had my lime and lemon drink been 'spiked' at the restaurant, and if so, why? (I have never been a drinker or a smoker or tried any drugs.) Within seconds, to my astonishment, but not causing any panic or increased heart rate on my part, there began to appear in front of me what looked like an Oriental man. I felt what I can only describe as an overall feeling of warmth and great happiness. My bedroom was filled with a beautiful, brilliant, golden light. The walls and the furniture were no longer visible, I was no longer aware of myself, just aware of this man, surrounded by a shining, bright light. As I watched in awe, he became clearer and clearer until he was as solid as you or I. He was the oldest person I had ever seen and yet he looked so youthful. I was shown two images of his face in that through the wrinkles I saw a younger version of this man. I could clearly see all the features of his face; he had thick white eyebrows and long white eyelashes. His moustache and beard were like white silk, the moustache being visible over the beard, which was the width of his chin and tapered to his waist. His hair was white and hung in a pigtail down his back. His eyes were his most shining feature. They were not like the eyes of the spirit children I had seen or like the eyes of any human I had met. The eyes were the focus of my attention. They shone out as if to tell the story of his whole being. They sparkled and twinkled with the pale blue of the rainbow. He looked so gentle and kind; and he oozed love and goodness. He wore a long gown which covered him from his neck to his feet, with a sash at the waist. It looked to me as if it was made of different shades of silver tinsel. It was shimmering, glowing and vibrating; in its whirling and spinning, seemed to be pulsating with life. His hands were hidden, each pushed up inside the opposite sleeve. A small, mandarin-style hat perched on top of his head. He was small and slim. I could not tell if he was standing on the floor or somehow suspended in mid-air.

It was not just this first experience of seeing this man that was so amazing but also the atmosphere of complete happiness and peace he created. Time could have stopped for me, there and then; I felt complete. Without question I could have severed all earthly ties and gone with him, if he had asked. I knew that I was in the presence of an angel. He bowed, and looking straight into my eyes, gave me a smile that made me feel that I wanted to be with this man forever. Without opening his mouth, his words filled my heart and mind. He said, "At last, my friend, it has taken time ...". With these words he faded and the room came back to normal. I sat motionless for a while, feeling depleted and weak. For some reason, I felt no need to question what had happened at that time. I was not disturbed or alarmed, but still felt relaxed. The whole experience had been acceptable to me. It took a lot of effort to undress and get myself into bed. I fell asleep quickly and as far as I remember had a good night's sleep.

I awoke to a whole new world; I felt like I had been chopped in half! It seemed to me that winter had come early; the colours of the earth had faded and everything looked so dull. Overnight my nature had altered; I had lost my jolly personality and my proud feeling of being physically fit - I was not myself. Over the next few days I felt that something was lacking in my life, I was swimming against the tide and felt the burden of everyday life. I could not face going to work (I worked in a timber yard at the time) - that seemed so trivial. I felt flat and yet became acutely aware of my surroundings. I saw everything in a fresh light. I noticed, for the first time, the shapes in my room. I was amazed at the defined lines, the sharpness of the corners on the furniture, window and door. It had never before entered my mind to study the details of my room. I had never looked at it in this way before, but had taken it all for granted.

I looked out of the window and into the garden. The pigeon loft, which I had previously admired as a feature of the garden, now looked like an old shed perched on a pile of bricks; I became aware, for the first time, of the space between the floor and the shed. The lush, green hedge became just a partition to separate us from the neighbours. The whole garden looked like it had been constructed from a Lego kit. Nothing blended together as before; I saw paving slabs, rose trees, shrubs and fences as individual items. Nothing looked permanent; it was as though everything had been placed there for the day.

As I looked further, beyond my garden, I saw the gaps between the houses, rather than the houses themselves. Through these gaps I saw the poplar trees which, in regimental fashion, lined the boundaries of the park. It looked, to me, as though these had been pushed into the ground overnight. The road looked like a trough purposely sunken into the earth, below ground level with the kerbstone dividing the cars from the pedestrians.

I was suddenly bombarded with the realisation that man was "squaring off" his own space, creating dividing lines, partitions and boundaries. I saw my world as if from an aerial view. It looked so artificial and sectioned, with little colour. Man was creating barriers but I knew that he was defenceless and could not hide.

As I thought more about my latest experience and my new

view of the world, albeit temporary, I became very confused and yet told no-one. As I tried to work things out, I knew that I could no longer dismiss the things that had been happening to me. From childhood I had always been pulled by religion and never understood why. I enjoyed RE lessons at school; I loved the simplicity of Jesus and all the Bible stories. I did not have the urge or opportunity to study the Bible in depth until much later in life. Whenever I went to church, for a family baptism, wedding or funeral, I remember thinking, and still do, that I would like to do that job (as a priest); or was I yearning for explanations, thinking that the church was the place with all the answers for me? I used to go with an inbuilt knowledge, from my gifts. I realised that there was such a lot left out of these services. There was so much that I could have shared with people. At a funeral, for instance, all that emotion when those who had passed on had long gone to the heavenly mansions, their reunions and celebrations being a week old. I had so much to tell, yet felt that no-one, especially my family, would understand. I was now confident in the knowledge, as I had long suspected, that I was gifted and privileged and that this could only have come from God. I had reached a turning point, both physically and spiritually, in my life and it was time to investigate.

Still in my late teens, I was preparing for an adventure in my life, which was completely out of character and a perfect example of my head ruling my heart; this adventure was to take me to North Africa. I was sitting in the garden, pondering on the outcome of my trip, when my guardian angel appeared before me, for the second time. I, again, looked round wondering if my mother could see us from the kitchen window. On this occasion the sensation was not so overwhelming, his dress was not as 'illuminated' as before. With the same smile and gentle bow, he clasped his hands together, looked straight at me, and said, " I am with you, because I choose ... You are greatly loved, but would dare to tread where I dare not. My prayers are for you and you cause us, on this side, much anguish." I understood this message to mean that he would not be able to communicate with me during my trip.

On my return, having come to terms with these visits, I decided to look for help. I wanted to ask so much of him and his

21

visits were so brief. I began to seek out people with similar experiences. Every Saturday, the *Birmingham Mail* advertised Spiritualist Church meetings at Digbeth Civic Hall - I decided to go. I managed to find the room where the meeting was being held; not knowing what to expect, I sheepishly went inside and was greeted by a very saintly-looking gentleman. He was about seventy years old and very smartly dressed. He shook my hand in a friendly manner, which I felt to be sincere. I paid an admission charge and was given a raffle ticket. In my daydreams I had imagined the room to be dimly lit by candles, with chairs arranged in a circle and full of Merlin-type characters or people dressed in black. The room was actually set out like a chapel, with chairs either side of the aisle and an altar at the front covered with flowers. I went to sit at the back of the room and I remember thinking, as I flicked through the prayer book, that if the people started holding hands I would have to leave. I had deliberately placed myself near the door, in case I had to make a quick escape. I had decided to try not to get into conversation, but to act as an observer at this stage. Before telling anyone about myself, I had to discover if these people were genuine. I became aware of the gentleman, who had greeted me at the door, looking at me. I turned and feeling rather embarrassed, smiled at him; he immediately came over to me. He introduced himself to me and said how lovely it was to see me at the meeting. I thanked him and with that he returned to his seat. I felt a little out of order in that I had purposely not given him my name. When most of the seats had been filled, a couple came out of a side room, walked onto the platform and stood behind the altar. The man opened with a prayer and then we all sang a hymn. The lady was introduced as the medium for the evening. After about fifteen minutes of "does anyone know Tom, or Bill, or Ada", etc. I quietly got up and left the room. I was followed by the old gentleman. He asked if this was my first visit to a spiritualist meeting; I told him that it was and that it would be my last. I felt really disappointed. He smiled at me and asked for me to wait a couple of minutes. He returned with a programme of events for this Spiritualist Church, listing these so-called mediums. He underlined the ones he thought to be credible. He asked me to come again and I agreed. I made a mental note of the first date, which was about three weeks away.

Before this next spiritualist meeting, my guardian angel visited me for the third time. I was at home, in my bedroom, and this happened whilst I was thinking about a few things I now regretted doing. This time he came in all his glory, dressed in a magnificent long, blue robe. The colour almost defies description - brighter than the bluest summer sky you have ever seen! I could almost hear the movement of his garments. Again my feelings and sensations were not of this world. I now knew, from experience, that this meeting would be short, and so I had prepared some key questions. I needed to know who he was and where he came from. I asked, "Who are you?" He answered, "My name is of no importance, but to give you proof that I am with you, my name is Su Leng." (I presume that this is the correct spelling.) "We have much work to do." I was so excited that I was able to have a conversation with him. "What sort of work?", I asked. "Like a flower that opens gently - so shall you", he replied. "Have you seen Jesus?" I asked. "I, myself, have not, but there are those, over this side, who have. God bless you, my friend. God bless you!" With that he disappeared.

I now knew his name and naturally wondered all about him. As for the work he spoke about - the only work I understood was working for a living, i.e. physical work. I had yet to realise the meaning of his symbolic language. Much more importantly, however, I felt that within seconds I had been given the answer to life! Jesus did exist at the centre of the heavenly realms. Su Leng, even though he could not admit to having seen Jesus, knew of people who had. I had wondered for so long, having heard the stories of Jesus at school and church, and suddenly I now knew it all to be true. All at once my fears were allayed and everything tied in for me. The existence of life after death was, to me, as normal a part of life as eating and sleeping; I knew that passing out of this life was just a transition, but I had been given more than faith; the barrier of doubt had been smashed. I had been given the evidence for believing - I had, no longer, to rely on blind faith. The seed had been sown - this experience created in me a yearning to investigate and study the birth, life, death and resurrection of Jesus Christ.

I now had a much more intimate relationship with Su Leng than I ever imagined possible.

October came and I was keen to go to the spiritualist meeting. I met the old gentleman there again; he was really happy to see me and I felt very comfortable with him. I sat in the corner, at the back of the room. All the seats were filled, this medium must have been popular, and so I struggled to see the altar. A man led a very ordinary-looking woman on to the platform. As before, the man opened with a prayer and then we all sang a hymn. The medium stood up and I could only see the top of her head - but that was enough! Her aura was a beautiful pale yellow with a tinge of pastel blue, as in the colours of the rainbow. She stood motionless for a moment, staring into space, as if she had forgotten her words. She moved across to the opposite side of the stage and in a loud voice, much more powerful than her size would suggest, she said, "I want the young man at the back of the room." The old gentleman had been putting extra chairs behind my row and so I was no longer sitting at the back. Even so, I was getting rather hot and embarrassed when she again asked for the young man at the back of the room - against the wall! So I sat up straight. "Yes," she said, "You!" "Me?" I stuttered. "Yes, my lad, you! Tonight you will no longer be a doubting Thomas. I have a Chinese gentleman with me who wishes for me to give you proof, so that you will get on and fulfil the gifts that God has bestowed upon you." Everyone was, by now, looking round at me. "You are privileged to have met your guide and, further more, you know his name. He wishes for me to give you his name this evening. You are so sensitive and of pure body and mind. You have brought much happiness to the House of Leng. Su Leng is proud to be using you as an instrument, in order to work many truths, and to give you the power of healing. Although you have many sufferings to endure, you will come to that day when you will work in service to Almighty God!"

I felt myself blushing and I was, understandably, close to tears. As I had never spoken to anyone about my experiences, I wanted to know all about this woman and how she could possibly have known all about me. This was way beyond my expectations! I had been so frustrated for so long and so to have all this confirmed, and in such detail, was a great comfort to me. My old gentleman kindly ushered me away from a dozen, or more, people, all bombarding me

24

with questions and asking me to join their 'circles'. I sensed that he was himself rather special; even so, he humbled himself and asked me if I had understood what I had been told. I definitely had, but still had many more questions. He was drawn to me and over the years became a great friend to me, helping and guiding me within this new world.

Even though I did not regularly attend spiritualist meetings, I was told again, in London and in Scotland, the name of my guide. Again these mediums were not known to me and neither could they have known anything about me.

Years later, after many personal trials, I was given the greatest gift of all. I needed to know where Su Leng came from; what and where was this other side of life of which he spoke. This burning question was now, finally, answered for me. I was now growing older, with many responsibilities and thus "physically" preoccupied with life. I had realised that conditions had to be right (with me) for Su Leng to come to me. I needed to be at peace with myself, i.e. in a relaxed state. This was rare and hard for me to achieve at this stage in my life. One late afternoon, however, as I sat exhausted on my own at home - Su Leng appeared to me. I took the opportunity to ask him, "Where, on this other side, are you from and is it possible for me to see this place?" Over a period of time, my wish was granted, and on three occasions I was able to leave my physical body, escorted by Su Leng, and have a look at the Spirit World. These were out-of-body experiences unlike those I had in the physical world. I had no floating sensation and I have no recollection of leaving my body. I was transferred directly out of my body to the Spirit World. When I arrived at this other side, on the first two occasions, it was so bright that I could not open my eyes. I had no fear and yet I was still thinking in the physical. The strange thing was that even though I was in the spirit I still needed to adjust to this other side. I was able to sense where I was; I could hear voices asking me to open my eyes - but I could not.

On the third visit I opened my eyes and I was able to see. I have heard many an explanation of what 'heaven' might be like - the reality was far beyond anything that I could ever have imagined. It is so hard to describe and explain what I saw - words cannot possibly do it justice. A physical being could not look upon this place - he would not be able to accept or comprehend what he saw. This image lives deep in my memory within, i.e. inside my spirit body. This is the 'thorn' in my side, that I feel that I cannot possibly, satisfactorily describe what I saw - it was too much! Imagine all the pleasure, happiness and good memories of a lifetime melted down and poured out before you. There is no comparison; yet, humbly, here goes:

The light was a beautiful pale yellow and was all around me. I could see far into the distance - there did not appear to be an horizon. I felt warm - but the warmth did not come from the sun; it was more like an inner glow all over my body. The garden that I was in contained the most beautiful flowers that I have ever seen, the colours were so bright that I could not identify them as dark or light. The colours of the rainbow were vivid and all around. There was no breeze or wind. I got the feeling that there was so much going on - somewhere! The place was vibrating with life and yet all was silent - in an inexplicable atmosphere. This was my own personal guided tour; all for my benefit. I was made aware of what I needed to see.

There was no moon or sun, or sky. The floor was not solid, but soft, like a cushioned floor. As I walked along it gave under foot - like a sponge; the floor felt as though it was covered by the most luscious and very, very thick pile carpet. It was so comfortable and of course there was no sound of footsteps. There were many trees all around me, they were all in full bloom and looked perfect. They were not weathered or splintered, and there was no decay, no cracks in the bark. There was not a bent or broken branch or twig, no fallen leaves. I recognised the species of trees: poplars, sycamore and birch. Each stood out magnificently against the yellow background in vivid shades of green and blue, rich ivory in the case of the birch trees. There was no lawn, but masses of flowers. The garden was not landscaped - no borders or hedges; great sections of flowers intermingled with each other, giving off a kaleidoscope of colour. Flowers of different varieties and seasons grew together, not one was hidden behind another. As with the trees, not one was bent over or facing downwards. I could walk amongst these flowers and cause no damage. I knew all these flowers and yet I dare not pick one! I could not smell the perfume of the flowers and yet I could smell water. I definitely sensed that there was water nearby and yet I never saw any. I could not imagine rushing water washing away the sands of time in this peaceful, motionless world.

Throughout the visit, Su Leng was by my side. I saw a couple of other people; they walked passed me and away into the distance. They wore long, white robes with a coloured sash around the waist: one purple and one blue. I realised that these people were being shown to me to give me the proof that this was a place of existence for spirit people.

I had such a feeling of utter bliss, the happiness I felt was overwhelming. I had no aches or pains and felt no urge to sniff, cough, blink or go to the toilet. I felt as though I was naked and yet when I looked down at my body I was covered in a white shroud.

Away from the garden I saw marble-coloured Roman-style buildings with huge pillars. Some of these were great halls of learning. I was led inside one of these halls; it was open and airy and I saw no shadows. I saw great long banqueting tables, made from the same material as the buildings. There were books, parchments and scrolls arranged in a very neat and tidy fashion down the middle of each table. The books were bound in a material that I did not recognise. I was invited to take a closer look, but did not touch anything.

The other buildings were hospitals. As with the halls of learning, there were no doors or windows. I was not allowed to look inside any of these hospitals. I listened intently, however, as Su Leng explained to me that these places were for depleted spirits, for example, of miscarriages, young children, abortions, and those who lived in a vegetative state on earth. Depleted spirits are those which have not been able to evolve within their earthly bodies; they have remained dormant because of the condition of the physical body and therefore denied their natural personality and experience of life on earth. At death, these spirits are met by highly-evolved spirits, or angels, and taken to one of these hospitals. As these spirits are without any record of earthly deeds, they are therefore unable at this time to progress or make their natural transition to one of the mansions. I was assured that because these spirits had not gained any experience of earthly life, they remained pure as they had no experience of sin. They are therefore put under the guidance of these guardian angels simply because they are outside of the natural law of the great plan. These spirits then undergo a divine process of rejuvenation and education within these halls of learning and hospitals. Jesus said,

"Why should you be envious because I am generous? Thus, the last will be first, and the first last." (Matthew 20:16)

Here we have real justice as heavenly riches are bestowed upon these spirits; herein lies their reward and compensation. Jesus also said,

"Let the little children come to me; do not stop them; for it is to such as these that the kingdom of God belongs. In truth I tell you, anyone who does not welcome the kingdom of God like a little child will never enter it." (**Mark 10:14-15**)

I finally plucked up the courage to ask, "What is this place, where am I?" Su Leng answered, "In our Father's house are many mansions. This is but only one." At this stage I did not understand what he was talking about. I now know this to be a quote from the Bible (See **St. John 14:2**).

For the duration of my visit I was aware of another person. Wherever I went, I could see a man to my right; as I walked, he walked; when I stopped, he stopped, always maintaining a set distance between us. I was so amazed and overwhelmed by what I was seeing and yet a little frustrated by this presence. It was as though he was 'sizing me up'; he watched my every move. I was obviously drawn to him and when we finally came face to face, I instinctively knew who he was. He silently acknowledged that I was correct in my assumption and yet when I asked him who he was, he answered, "For the purpose I am Abdullah." I am not at liberty to divulge his true identity, but I can reveal that this man walked through the Old Testament. I knew this man and he knew me!

I had out-of-body experiences in the physical world and my silver cord was still visible to me. When I was taken to see the Spirit World, I was transported in a flash! I was not 'taken up', i.e. to heaven above, and I did not travel through a tunnel, as those who had near-death experiences have described. I had such a gradual introduction to this other world - I could not open my eyes until the third visit. Even though my cord was obviously still connected to me, it was not visible - because my spirit body was in its natural, rightful home -

where it belongs! I must stress that I felt very much 'at home' in the Spirit World; I had a definite sense of belonging. I do not know which particular mansion I visited, however. The Spirit World is not as far away as you would imagine, not way into space, but all around us. The Spirit World is the aura of our world, vibrating around and within it, enveloping it and yet intermingling with it. The spirit realms penetrate straight through our world, and yet are invisible to most.

As you can imagine, it took a long time for me to recover from this incredible adventure. I, and the world, would never be the same again - the earth seems so diluted and little impresses me now! Through all this, I had gained so much, yet lost so much. By being shown the Spirit World, I had the highest privilege bestowed upon me. As each spiritual gift was revealed to me I was given more proof, but this experience gave me the ultimate proof, of the existence of the rainbow mansions.

Chapter 3
"NATURAL TRANSITION"

I am now going to explain the many mansions of the spirit world. Let us imagine the spirit world as a rainbow wheel. There are seven rings, known as mansions, from the outer red, blending into orange, yellow, green, blue, indigo and finally to violet. At the heart of this wheel is the heavenly Jerusalem, where the light is many times more powerful than the sun. The major religions teach us that there are only two places of existence in the afterlife: the extremes of HELL, for the undesirables, and HEAVEN, for the good and righteous. They offer no explanation for anything in between. In actual fact there are seven, leading to the heavenly Jerusalem. The colours in the aura reveal natural personality and therefore give a self-judgement. I understand that the seven mansions, represented by the colours of the rainbow, correspond to these colours. So, at death, there is a natural transition, from this world to the spirit world, according to the colour in the aura, in life.

Yellow is, for me, the dividing colour between good and bad. The outer mansion is the red, most definitely a place of torment and guilt, known as hell by some, for those who have been the most evil on earth. The Bible talks of many being "cast out", i.e. to this outer mansion. The orange mansion is for those who have been evil on earth; they are aware of their crimes and are willing - and then allowed - to repent. From the yellow, there is a definite progression, working towards the light, i.e. the heavenly Jerusalem. Jesus talks of entering these mansions through gates. He says,

"Enter ye in at the strait gate: for wide is the gate, and broad is the way, that leadeth to destruction, and many there be which go in thereat. Because strait is the gate, and narrow is the way, which leadeth into life, and few there be that find it." (Matthew 7:13-14)

For me, the best explanation of the mansions is given in the parable of the rich man and Lazarus. This is the only parable, throughout the gospels, in which Jesus names his characters: Dives, Lazarus and Abraham. In my opnion this was done to get the attention of the crowd, including the Pharisees. He lifts their thoughts onto a higher spiritual level by using father Abraham in the story, who was the forefather of the Jewish religion. In simple terms, he gives us an insight into the two extremes of the mansions.

The rich man used to dress in purple and feast magnificently every day. He never wanted for anything, was a very selfish man and thought of no-one but himself. He lived only for what the day would bring. On the other hand, there was a beggar named Lazarus. He was very poor and could not afford fine linen. He was so poor that he could not afford to buy food and so he was undernourished, and because of his diet he was covered with sores. He longed to fill himself with that which fell from the rich man's table. Lazarus used to lie at the rich man's gate. The rich man never noticed him, he only looked as far as his own table. The dogs would come and lick the sores on the body of this poor man and even though Lazarus was a beggar, he was not a sinful man. He was just one of life's tragedies - and the rich man ignored his tragic plight. In time they both died. In the afterlife the rich man found himself in a place of torment and guilt. He was burning up with guilt and remorse, he was tortured by his own anger as he remembered his sinful life on earth. All his memories were painful and he had no rest. Lazarus was carried away by angels as his spirit was so depleted. He found himself in a place, in the embrace of Abraham. Abraham talked to Lazarus, telling him that his worries were now over, his sores all healed and that he would suffer no more. His hunger pains were all gone and he had gained a far greater feast, compared with anything seen on the rich man's table. So here we have sinfulness and righteousness; the rich man in a place of torment, Lazarus in a place of peace. The rich man looked out from where he was and, a long way off, he saw Abraham talking with Lazarus. He cried out to Abraham,

"Father Abraham, let Lazarus come here to me so that I can apologise to him. I want to tell him how sorry I am for the way I treated him. I want to put things right between us - for I am in agony and burning up with guilt. If I can do this, perhaps I will feel better." Abraham answered, "My son, during your life on earth you had everything, but Lazarus had nothing; you are in agony and he is at peace. There is a great gulf between you. I cannot allow Lazarus to come to you, it is not possible, and you cannot come to us, that is

31

also not possible." The rich man cried out to Abraham once more, "Father Abraham, please, I beg you! If you cannot help me, then send Lazarus to my father's house, where I have five brothers, all leading immoral, sinful lives - just as I was doing. If Lazarus could go to them, he could tell them about this place of torment; they could change their ways and avoid coming here." Abraham answered, "If they do not listen to Moses and the prophets about living a moral life, then they will not be convinced even if someone should rise from the dead, to tell them." (See Luke16:19-31)

Let us now examine this story very closely. We have the rich man on one level, the red ring, i.e. the outer mansion, and Lazarus on a much higher level, with Abraham. There is a great gulf between them, containing other mansions. According to Abraham, it is not possible to pass from any of the other mansions to the outer mansion, or to ever escape from the torment and guilt of the outer mansion. Therefore, the rich man cannot visit Lazarus and vice versa:

" ... a great gulf has been fixed, to prevent those who want to cross from our side to yours or from your side to ours." **(Luke 16:26)**

However, when the rich man asks for Lazarus to visit his brothers on earth, Abraham does not dismiss this idea. I therefore understand that in this case there would be no restriction on crossing from the spirit world to earth. The Old Testament teaches, and Abraham quotes from this, that the Israelites, time and time again, turned their backs on the law of Moses and God's word, i.e. to lead a moral and sinless life. The story gives the example of the rich man as a selfish glutton. However, his crimes were not the most offensive known to man and Lazarus was a victim of his time. Jesus had no choice but to use these examples because of the cynicism and hypocrisy of the crowd and the Pharisees. The rich man represented the Pharisees and Lazarus represented the crowd. The rich man is the example of one who enters by the wide gate and Lazarus the example of one who enters by the narrow gate. Jesus tells us that it is much harder to be good and follow the rules; many will enter by the wide gate and few by the narrow gate. Jesus says,

"I am the gate. Anyone who enters through me will be safe." **(St John 10:9)**

I take this to mean that anyone who follows the example of

Jesus will enter the mansions through a much narrower gate.
He continues,

" ... *such a one will go in and out and will find pasture.*" (St
John 10:9)

When the natural transition has been made and we arrive at
the rainbow mansions, we carry with us "the record of our deeds".
We have to realise, first and foremost, that although we have died
and passed from the physical to the spirit world, we are, in fact, still
alive. Some find this harder to accept than others. Now is the time
to take stock and face up to our life on earth. By looking back
objectively at our lives we will start our progression through the
mansions. Now is the time to truly acknowledge and then confess our
sins. In doing so, we will be able to move on. Certain actions may
need explanation. We will be able to face up to the burdens and
regrets of our lives once and for all. Those fellow spirits who were
the victims of our actions will confront us at last, and vice versa.
There will be no way out as we realise that there was never any
excuse or justification for our wrongdoings. However, we will not be
alone in this learning process - higher evolved spirits will help to
solve each problem as it arises. This process is part of the divine
plan. So much of our life is already mapped out and now is the time
to look back and decide what was predestined or out of our hands
and what could have been altered or diverted. Now is the time to
judge yourself. Progression can be slow as the greatest sins are dealt
with first. When all the shadows are cast off and we realise right
from wrong, we are then free to look at the good in ourselves - free
to progress.

At death we are drawn to the light. As we progress through
the mansions, this light becomes brighter and brighter. The light is a
reflection of God's glory. As spirits we will move involuntarily, in
stages, as we develop. Movement within the mansions is allowed
from the inner to the outer rings. It must be a two-way process, if one
spirit wishes to visit another, i.e. from one level to another. For
example, if a battered wife is called by her husband, it has to be by
her consent that they meet again. Through spiritual understanding
and progress, the time will come when they will both be able to
accept that the love of the spirit has no malice. Reunions within

33

families or friends may be more commonplace (as on earth).

Let us now look at the different ways in which we pass from the physical to the spirit world. St Paul says,

"Now I am going to tell you a mystery: we are not all going to fall asleep, but we are all going to be changed, instantly, in the twinkling of an eye ..." **(1 Co 15:51-52)**

The most natural way, and time, to pass is at old age. The silver cord grows thinner and thinner and severs ever so gently. The transition in this case is certainly without problems and according to God's natural law. This is the most straightforward passing.

When a child passes they will not have lived many years and so this is not according to natural law. I refer to children 0-12 years who have experienced some life, but who have not yet reached puberty. As they enter the spirit world, they are met by a relative who has passed over, who was known to them in life. They help them to adjust, i.e. to realise that they have passed over. As these children pass at such a tender age, they will not have been exposed to much vice. As they are, therefore, pure in that respect, they will inherit a higher status within the many mansions. Higher evolved spirits help them to progress, until they reach maturity, i.e. their prime (28-30 years in earth terms). This also works, in reverse, for older spirits who, as they progress, come back into their prime.

"At this time the disciples came to Jesus and said, 'Who is the greatest in the kingdom of Heaven?' So he called a little child to him whom he set among them. Then he said, 'In truth I tell you, unless you change and become like little children you will never enter the kingdom of Heaven. And so, the one who makes himself as little as this little child is the greatest in the kingdom of Heaven'" **(Matthew 18:1-5)**

Premature death also comes with violence or accident - again this is not a natural way to die. With a sudden death, the spirit is catapulted out of the body at great speed, and is in a state of shock. The cord is instantly cut off, having had no time to sever gently. In this case, the spirit is not drawn to the light, but retains immediate memory and therefore remains tied to the earth - caught in-between the earth and the spirit world. There is a much greater adjustment to be made. The spiritual and physical have become entwined and need

34

time to unravel. Spirits are often spotted at the scene of the accident or crime (death). They cannot let go of their earthly ties, cannot believe that they have died! I have seen many of these "hauntings", because of my "gift" and Su Leng has explained this all to me. As in life, all depends on the personality of the victim. Highly evolved spirits come radiating love, warmth and peace, to break down this barrier of isolation. It is in their power to dissolve these earthly ties, reveal the light, where a loved one will be waiting, and the transition will take place.

One of the strangest experiences I ever had was in 1979, when I was living in Yorkshire. I was dealing with some paperwork to do with my business when I was disturbed by a voice. It was the voice of a young boy, who had passed over and was obviously in some distress. I had previously experienced hearing voices crying for help but, not knowing what to do, had closed my mind to them and they had simply faded away. This time I felt so strongly that this boy had somehow attached himself to me, that I would have to help him. Eventually the voice came as clear as though he were sitting in the room with me and we were able to have a conversation. The boy had been killed in the Blitz and was distressed about his dog. The dog was a black and white Border Collie, given to him by his grandfather as it had been unsuccessful as a sheepdog. The dog had been left at home, while the boy visited his grandmother. His mother had gone to fetch some dark curtains. There was an air raid; suddenly the house shook and he felt a freezing sensation and saw a flash of what he thought was lightening. He had been looking for his dog ever since. The boy said that he had heard the dog barking several times, but could not figure out where the sound was coming from. He asked me if I had got his dog. I understood the boy's situation; as he had suffered such a sudden death in the bomb blast and was so obsessive about finding his dog, his young spirit was in shock, and he was preventing himself from entering the many mansions. I needed help as this was not something I had experienced before. My thoughts were to keep the boy talking and I hoped that either Su Leng or someone from the "other side" would help and tell me what to do. I asked the boy's name. It was Stanley and he explained that everyone called him by that name, except for his grandfather. Within a split second of his mentioning his grandfather, I heard the voice of an old gentleman. He thanked me for being so patient with the boy and explained that when he had given the dog to his grandson, the boy had insisted on giving it the same name as the nickname given to him by his grandfather.

"Tell him I've got Chief here with me", he said.

"Stanley, I know where Chief is and who he is with", I said.

Stanley replied, "I knew that you had got him, because I heard him barking around you!"

For the next ten minutes or so, I witnessed the greatest reunion between a boy and his grandfather, and a boy and his dog. (My profession at this time was a greyhound trainer and in my care I had, in kennels, sixty greyhounds.)

I have always known of the existence of the animal kingdom within the many mansions. This episode with "Chief" gave yet more proof that spirits can be with their pets in the spirit world.

Isaiah, like others of the C8 BC - Amos, Hosea, Micah, was essentially a prophet of doom and judgement. Yet it is to Isaiah that we turn for the best biblical reference to the animal kingdom within the many mansions.

"The wolf also shall dwell with the lamb, and the leopard shall lie down with the kid; and the calf and the young lion and the fatling together; and a little child shall lead them. And the cow and the bear shall feed; their young ones shall lie down together: and the lion shall eat straw like the ox. And the sucking child shall play on the hole of the asp, and the weaned child shall put his hand on the cockatrice' den. They shall not hurt nor destroy in all my holy mountain: for the earth shall be full of the knowledge of the Lord, as the waters cover the sea. And in that day there shall be a root of Jesse, which shall stand for an ensign of the people; to it shall the Gentiles seek: and his rest shall be glorious." **(Isaiah 11:6-10)**

The description of the animal kingdom is one of complete peace and harmony. This could not be achieved on earth, but is only possible with God in the heavenly mansions. The root of Jesse represents Christ himself. He is the flagship, he draws all people to him, to the many mansions. Isaiah goes on to say:

"And the Lord shall utterly destroy the tongue of the

Egyptian sea; and with his mighty wind shall he shake his hand over the river, and shall smite it in the seven streams, and make men go over dry-shod. And there shall be an highway for the remnant of his people, which shall be left, from Assyria; like as it was to Israel in the day that he came up out of the land of Egypt." **(Isaiah 11:15-16)**

The wind, translated from the Hebrew, means Spirit of God. The seven streams are symbolic for the seven colours of the rainbow and seven mansions; the highway represents the highway of progression through the many mansions.

Life can also be cut short in the case of suicide. When this happens, for whatever reason, there is no escape. When a person takes his own life, intentionally, he will still have to face the consequences. He will still make the transition to the spirit world, drawn to his natural place, within the many mansions, but find himself with others who have taken their own lives - like attracts like in the spirit world. Progression will be stunted as the suicide will be the first thing to be dealt with, in the process of self-judgement. The greatest shock will be that even though he has left the physical world, he is now "living" in the spirit world. In this atmosphere of love and harmony, he will be helped to look back at his life and the possible alternatives to his action. I quote the Bible on this subject:

"And there came out of the smoke locusts upon the earth: and unto them was given power, as the scorpions of the earth have power. And it was commanded them that they should not hurt the grass of the earth, neither any green thing, neither any tree, but only those men which have not the seal of God in their foreheads. And to them it was given that they should not kill them; but that they should be tormented five months: and their torment was as the torment of a scorpion, when he striketh a man. And in those days shall men seek death, and shall not find it, and shall desire to die, and death shall flee from them" **(Revelation 9:3-6)**

As I have already mentioned, as spirits evolve, they naturally revert or develop into their "prime". Any illness or disability of the physical body will naturally disappear on entering the spirit world. The spirit body is free of all afflictions and can leave them all behind. The lame will walk, the deaf will hear, the blind will see; there will be no sickness or pain. The physical body is made up of

37

matter, i.e. it occupies space and has mass. The spirit body, on the other hand, can pass through matter in the physical world. In its own environment, the spirit world being a higher vibration of life, the spirit body takes control and takes on a comfortable form. As the spirit world is a world of thought, movement is at will, so the shape or form of the spirit body is of no consequence (except for recognition). The further it progresses towards the centre, the less the spirit takes with it. There will be no need for a body shape as we know it and our physical body will become just a memory.

Jesus gave the following description of the heavenly mansions to St John:

"And God shall wipe away all tears from their eyes; and there shall be no more death, neither sorrow nor crying, neither shall there be any more pain: for the former things are passed away." **(Revelation 21:4)**

Jesus demonstrates on earth what is to be in the spirit world. Isaiah talks of a promise of things to come:

"And in that day shall the deaf hear the words of the book, and the eyes of the blind shall see out of obscurity, and out of darkness" **(Isaiah 29:18)**

Isaiah in using "book" is referring to Christ. This symbolism reappears in Revelation when St John speaks of the "Book of Life".

The gospel of Matthew says:

"The blind receive their sight, and the lame walk, the lepers are cleansed, and the deaf hear, the dead are raised up, and the poor have the gospel preached to them." **(Matthew 11:5)**

In the spirit world there is no need for speech or language; there will be no language barrier. As we make our natural transition and go through periods of adjustment and progression, we will gradually realise that the voice and language are no longer necessary. We will communicate by thought and telepathy. (It will only be in the lower mansions where voices will be heard.) In this way, we will be able to communicate with more than one person at a time. All nations will therefore come together as all the barriers and prejudices disappear, e.g. those created by language. In the physical world, lies can be detected by a disturbance in the aura, creating disharmony between the physical and the spiritual. Similarly, when this happens in the

38

spirit world, a lie is automatically and instantly repelled and the conversation terminated. So, as we strive to become perfect, as we progress through the mansions, failings such as dishonesty will disappear.

I would now like to talk about near-death experiences, i.e. about those who **start** to make the transition. Many people have reported having near-death experiences, for example at the scene of an accident or on the operating table. They recall watching themselves being treated by doctors and nurses, even hearing their conversations. Some have spoken of being attached to a silver cord, as they hover above their own body. The person starts to die, and the spirit body starts to make the transition. Some have experienced shooting off, at great speed, towards a very bright light, others speak of a tunnel, or being drawn or sucked in a particular direction. On this journey towards the light, the further they go, the brighter the light becomes. They slow down and some are met by relatives or loved ones, others by angels. Most describe a place of happiness or bliss. They are then told that it is not their time yet and that they have to go back to the physical world. So the reverse happens and they wake up. The outward journey is towards death; resuscitation brings the spirit body back. If the resuscitation were not successful, the body would shut down, the cord would sever and that journey would continue into the spirit world. Many people return to good health, often with a positive change in personality and outlook. They are able at this point to take stock and appreciate life much more - many speak of becoming "more aware". Many describe their near-death experience as a religious or spiritual one and encounter a spiritual revival within themselves as a result. Most are reported as saying that death has now become something to look forward to, rather than something to fear; and some are disappointed that they have returned to this world.

Many terminally ill patients, having been in an almost vegetative state for some time, sometimes experience, as they approach death, what can only be described as a renewed surge of energy. Their eyes, which had been dull or even closed for many weeks, sparkle once more. Their facial expression shows complete comfort and joy and lights up with renewed awareness. The arms reach out after being limp for so long. They raise themselves up and call out to a loved one, who may have passed away many years before. Doctors and nurses often report that in patients about to make the transition and enter the famous valley of the shadow of death, that their faces change; they are happier, they cry out to loved ones, describe seeing a beautiful light and then pass in perfect peace. The most direct promise of this transition into the mansions, or spirit world, was recorded by St Luke, who was himself a physician. As Jesus hung on the cross between the two thieves, he said:

"Verily I say unto thee, Today shalt thou be with me in paradise." **(St Luke 23:43)**

A family friend, Angela Vora, a working nurse and wife of a GP, recalls this phenomenon:

"As a 14-year-old I always knew what I wanted to do when I left school. I wasn't influenced by anyone or anything; it was just something I instinctively knew. The training was long, or so I thought at the time, but from the beginning I worked on the wards and nursed people till they were better, or until they died."

"My first experience of death was whilst working on a ward for the elderly. These were expected deaths and many of the patients seemed glad to be, at last, 'meeting their maker'. For so long some had suffered the indignities of old age and infirmity. Some were unable to communicate because of deafness, blindness, dementia, or stroke. Life held no joys for them; lying in a hospital bed abandoned by families and friendless except for us, their nurses."

"Many had gone through two world wars losing husbands, sons and fathers. Their memories of those days were vivid and we heard many stories of deprivation, poverty, courage and fortitude. Each patient had their own tale to tell and we were privileged to hear them."

"My first experience of someone dying was a ninety-year-old lady who became my friend. I was seventeen. She had a cancerous growth which had spread all over her body. She had no family and she confided in us, knowing she did not have long to live. She became very weak and we all knew it would not be long. We cared for her, making her comfortable, relieving her pain with drugs. She became almost comatose and as I went off for my break I knew the

40

end was near."

"To my amazement, when I came back a half-an-hour later, she was awake and she was smiling. Colour had returned to her face and I was overjoyed, and in my naive way I thought she somehow had made a great improvement. Her eyes shone as she spoke of her dear husband who had died five years before her. Our spirits lifted and we marvelled at her recovery. We talked about what we would do the following day, as we washed her and put on her new nightdress we had bought for her. I brushed her hair and she smiled; she looked wonderful. I went to get her some fresh water to drink and as I returned I realised that she had died. I felt cheated and angry and talked to my senior nurse. She told me that this phenomenon was called the 'last light', when patients near to death get a sudden glow, a last surge of life before they depart. I've experienced it many times since and it is a wonderful thing to behold."

"Later on in my career I worked as a district nurse and one of my patients became very ill, having had multiple strokes. My colleagues and I visited three or four times a day to make sure he was comfortable. One night I sat with him so that his wife could get some sleep. He couldn't talk but we had nursed him long enough to know what he wanted. During that time we had discussed dying and I knew his fear was that of being alone when he died. His wife was devoted to him and she sat with him, talked to him, read to him, and prayed with him."

"We nurses would go in pairs to tend to him, having pre-arranged times to meet up. One day I was due to meet at 2 p.m. and I had gone for a swim in my lunch break. I had been in the water for about ten minutes when I suddenly knew I had to go to him. His wife was in the kitchen and was surprised to see me so early. I asked her to come with me to his bedside, which she did. She took his hand and he opened his eyes and smiled at her and then peacefully slipped away from us."

Having made this natural transition, spirits will often visit loved ones back on earth - to comfort or influence in times of need. For recognition, these spirits will appear in good health as they were remembered. For example, if a grandmother visits a sick child she will come in her old apron and slippers if this is how the child remembered her. This is done so that the visit does not shock or create a barrier of any kind between the two parties. When such a reunion takes place, the feelings of warmth and happiness that are experienced become the most vivid memory. At a family celebration, a wedding for example, spirit members of the family are able to 'gate-crash' and their images often captured on photographs. They dress for the occasion, as if in the physical, perhaps in a favourite suit or hat - again for recognition. I have met many people who have been overwhelmed by such meetings and I cannot recall anyone reporting that the spirit was unhappy.

The concept of time is apparently non-existent within the many mansions. There is eternal day and eternal summertime. Nothing is measured, or therefore governed, by time. The Bible says,

"For a thousand years in thy sight are but as yesterday when it is past, and as a watch in the night" **(Psalms 90:4)**

St Peter tells us,

"But, beloved, be not ignorant of this one thing, that one day is with the Lord as a thousand years, and a thousand years as one day." **(2 Peter 3:8)**

When a loved one makes the transition to the many mansions the grief and mourning for that person may last a lifetime. One question that is often asked is whether the deceased grieves in the spirit world. This can only be answered by looking at the time factor within the spirit world, i.e. that time is of no consequence now. There are no time limits on adjustment, reunions or progression. There is therefore, no opportunity for grieving for loved ones back on earth.

The Psalmist goes on to describe the time-span of life on earth:

"The days of our years are three score years and ten; and if by reason of strength they be four score years, yet is their strength labour and sorrow; for it is soon cut off, and we fly away." **(Psalms 90:10)**

After almost three thousand years this is still an accurate average, and if we can accept verse ten, we must therefore accept what he says in verse four which makes the comparison between 'time' on earth and in the spirit world. For me it illustrates the whole concept of a timeless spirit world. A thousand years on earth is but a day or night to God.

St Peter, about whom Jesus said,

"... thou art Peter, and upon this rock I will build my church ..." **(Matthew 16:18)** reminds us of this in the New Testament.

42

Chapter 4
"THE UNVEILING"

I have told you a little of my life story: of my spiritual gifts, my guardian angel Su Leng, my personal experience of the spirit world and of my yearning to study the Bible. Preoccupied with business and family, I had no time to read the Bible; a few years ago however, bedridden through illness, I finally got the opportunity to start these studies. I remember saying to my wife that I could not just lie in bed and do nothing but what could I do? "I know, I'll read that Bible", I thought. I had never questioned the existence of God and wanted to learn all about Jesus, having been drawn to the traditional Bible stories. At the spiritualist meetings I had never seen a Bible, so I naturally wondered if these two sides of my personality could ever meet in harmony. I had been given as a present a New Jerusalem Bible. It was frustrating at first; should I read the Old or the New Testament? As I recall, I read the gospels first, starting with John. I felt an instant connection - it was very exciting and quite emotional. It was like learning a new foreign language. As I read, I felt I was a part of this book - that I belonged; I could relate to what I was reading. I found the golden bowl, the silver cord, explanation and description of the spirit world and even the message from Su Leng - *"In my Father's house are many mansions"* ! (**St John 14:2**) I found many symbolic references to these many mansions. I remember shouting down to my wife, "It's all here!"

I found that I could give a deeper explanation of the words of Jesus than I had heard before, because of my insight and spiritual gifts. In all the gospel stories and the parables Jesus shared his knowledge and gave many clues in all he said. There was no mystery for me. I could no longer dismiss Jesus Christ - he preached about the spirit world, and in so doing, confirmed all that I knew. I was fulfilled. He spoke of a place I knew - a place that I had visited. I remember thinking at the time, "I *know* where I will be going when I die!" It brought everything together for me. I found a book within a book; a dual-purpose book for dual-purpose beings.

I had not been a scholar or an academic, or involved in worship or praising the Lord in public, but at this point I was drawn into the local Christian community, looking for answers. In discussion with friends at Church I realised that others did not see what I saw in the Bible; I offended people and I did not understand why. I came to prefer the King James' version; it speaks more accurately to me than the modern versions which at times, in my opinion, distort the word of God. I knew that there was an afterlife, was sure of the existence of the spirit world; I had that prior knowledge (and I am not alone in this) and I needed backup that God existed within the spirit realms. The Bible confirmed all that I knew - and more! I found it all in the Bible! I had suspected that I must be a little strange or weird, but when I read about Jesus I realised that I am just an ordinary man.

For me, the icing on the cake was when I came to the Book of Revelation (the last book of the New Testament), which is also known as the Apocalypse. In modern times, 'apocalypse' has come to denote some imminent worldwide catastrophe, but translated from the Greek it actually means 'unveiling'. Revelation was written by St. John the Divine, who was the youngest disciple. Jesus loved him very much and so it seems logical that this message, the revelation of Jesus Christ, should be delivered through him. John tells us of what he was shown in his vision. He was "in the Spirit on the Lord's day", i.e. worshipping and praising the Lord to the point of ecstasy. He went into a trance-like state and was therefore 'open' to experience this vision.

It begins with a 'summing-up' of the Old Testament, and the history of the Jews, reminding us of the sinfulness of man and how he turned his back on God. The Old Testament is made up of the old 'laws of threatening' - retribution for sins, real 'doom and gloom'. (When Jesus came he brought with him the new 'laws of mercy'.)

In Chapter 21, John is taken 'in the spirit' (in the ultimate out-of-body experience) for a glimpse of the future to see the heavenly Jerusalem, the top mansion, the heart of our rainbow wheel. John gives a detailed description of the heavenly Jerusalem and it is this section that upholds the Book of Revelation. I recognised this perfect place. Jesus showed John what is to come; what could not be achieved on earth will be achieved in heaven. Chapters 21 and 22 unlocked my secret - giving proof of the spirit world. He describes what I had seen and felt - no sun or moon, no pain or sorrow, the warmth, the light, etc. He shows us the future, which is not a paradise on earth but a paradise in heaven. Jesus tells us,

"My kingdom is not of this world: if my kingdom were of this world, then would my servants fight, that I should not be delivered to the Jews: but now is my kingdom not from hence. Pilate therefore said unto him, Art thou a king then? Jesus answered, Thou sayest that I am a king. To this end I was born, and for this cause I came into the world, that I should bear witness to the truth." **(St John 18:36-37)**

Jesus states that his kingdom is not, and will not be, part of this world; his kingdom is the spirit world. He does not say that he will come back in the future as ruler of a kingdom on this earth. He knows that he is going to die, that he has to die, i.e. 'come into his glory', to fulfil the scriptures and prophecies of the Old Testament. His purpose was to return to the heavens to prove that there is a resurrection, that we are all a dual purpose being and that we will all return as spirits to the many mansions.

Let us now look at Chapters 21 and 22:

The Book of Revelation has the reputation of being the most complicated and controversial book of the Bible. People are afraid of what it has to say, even theology lecturers and monks I have met, as it is so difficult for them to understand. We have to face up to it, without being put off by all the symbolic language.

I love the Book of Revelation - I can identify with its hidden message. Let us now look at it in more detail. Revelation tells us that the centre of our rainbow wheel is the heavenly Jerusalem, where reside God and his son, Jesus Christ. This place is the pulse and heartbeat for everything created in heaven and on earth. It is described in symbolic language to the very last detail, as a perfect construction. The city is described as the 'bride of the lamb'; the measurements and construction all representative of the twelve tribes of Israel. What a remarkable city this is! A perfect cube, the perimeter measuring 12,000 furlongs, (about 1,380 miles) surrounded by a wall 144 cubits (210 feet) in height. It would cover an area about 14 times that of modern Israel and tower almost 350 miles into space. It is a city devoid of any irregularity or defect. Even the foundation stones are beautiful, being adorned with twelve precious stones. This brings

45

to mind the Jewish high priest, who on ceremonial days wore an ephod studded with twelve different precious stones. This was the breastplate of judgement, the reminder of all the past sins of God's chosen people.

In the Book of Revelation we read of predictions of unprecedented horror, the details of which will only be fully revealed when a secret book is opened at the End of Days. This is the book sealed with seven seals which can only be opened by the Messiah himself.

"And I saw in the right hand of him that sat on the throne a book written within and on the backside, sealed with seven seals. And I saw a strong angel proclaiming with a loud voice, Who is worthy to open the book, and to loose the seals thereof? And no man in heaven, nor in earth, neither under the earth, was able to open the book, neither to look thereon" **(Revelation 5:1-4)**

"... the Lion of the tribe of Juda, the Root of David ..." (Jesus) *"... hath prevailed to open the book, and to loose the seven seals thereof."* **(Revelation 5:5)**

In the Book of Daniel we find the original version of this - an angel reveals the ultimate future to Daniel, a Hebrew prophet, and then tells him:

"But thou, O Daniel, shut up the words, and seal the book, even to the time of the end ..." **(Daniel 12:4)**

The early Christians believed that the New Testament clearly stated that the 'End' would come in their own lifetimes; for example, Christ warned:

"This generation shall not pass, till all these things be fulfilled". **(Matthew 24:34)**

In each successive age someone would emerge to predict that 'the End is nigh!' for example, at the close of the first millennium, at every time of war or crisis, etc. They would always quote the Bible, believing that they had solved the riddles in the symbolic language, thus enabling them to predict when the End was coming. They were always wrong.

I believe that the 'End of Time', or the 'End of Days' means the end of human life upon the earth. It would be impossible and stupid to predict when this might happen. Unless man alters his ways, protects his environment and ceases to wage war upon his fellow man, this threat could indeed be very close. It may be a natural disaster or Act of God on a huge scale, e.g. massive earthquake, volcano or flood, that contributes to the end of the world; or we may be wiped out by something way out of our control - a meteorite or asteroid hurtling in from outer space and colliding with the earth.

Sixty-five million years ago an asteroid, bigger than the largest mountain of the earth, struck the earth, exploding with the force of three hundred million hydrogen bombs and killed off all the dinosaurs. Was this a natural phenomenon or the hand of God? Scientists now agree that mankind could not have come into existence until the dinosaurs had been wiped out; they could not have co-existed.

I have already explained that the many mansions are a place of progression, that the starting point is according to one's earthly life and that there are restrictions in movement between the mansions. This brings together all the messages of the Bible that man must, at some point, be responsible for his actions, good or bad, and that there is a spiritual place of judgement, albeit self-judgement, designed by the Almighty.

"For we know that if our earthly house of this tabernacle were dissolved, we have a building of God, an house not made with hands, eternal in the heavens". (**2 Corinthians 5:1**)

"For we must all appear before the judgement seat of Christ; that every one may receive the things done in his body, according to that he hath done, whether it be good or bad". (**2 Corinthians 5:10**)

Let us now suppose that all human life on earth has been extinguished and that every spirit has returned to the many mansions, drawn to its rightful place to begin the progression towards the great light - the heavenly Jerusalem. It is impossible for me to say when, or if, each spirit will reach the great city. We are talking about infinity in the spirit world - a very difficult concept for us to understand:

"... and they shall reign for ever and ever." (**Revelation 22:5**)

Let us now return to the Book of Revelation, in particular Chapter 6 onwards, as in John's vision, Jesus opens the seven seals. These seals are opened one by one at the end of time, that is, when there is no more life on earth, when all the horrors of the human world have passed. As each seal is opened, we are given, symbolically, a picture of some devastation or injustice on earth; those spirits involved will now be held responsible. Their actions will determine their place within the many mansions and their rate of progression.

If we study these seals in terms of the rainbow wheel, then the seals to be opened run from the orange through to the violet: orange, yellow, green, blue, indigo and violet. The outer ring of the rainbow wheel is the red ring and as we have already established, will be left exactly as it is - for the most evil of spirits will never progress and must suffer a second death. The seventh seal must therefore symbolise the heavenly Jerusalem. The breaking of this final seal revealing the top mansion, breaking down all restrictions and barriers within the spirit world.

"And I saw when the Lamb opened one of the seals, and I heard, as it were the noise of thunder, one of the four beasts saying, Come and see. And I saw, and behold a white horse: and he that sat on him had a bow; and a crown was given unto him: and he went forth conquering, and to conquer." **(Revelation 6:1-3)**

Here, Jesus opens the first of the seals at the end of time. The earth is no more and everyone who has ever lived is now safely within the spirit realms. The spirit world, being of a higher vibration, is indestructible.

"... God our Saviour; who will have all men to be saved, and to come unto the knowledge of the truth." **(1 Timothy 2:3-5)**

Jesus is introduced by the mightiest of drum rolls, as he begins to reveal the future. The vision shows him riding a white horse, a symbol of holiness, righteousness and purity. His beautiful aura - the supreme aura - radiates with light a spectacular array of all the colours of the rainbow; each colour in his aura symbolising one of the many mansions. He will ride through the many mansions, displaying God's colours for all to see. He significantly dons the colours of the rainbow - representing the final judgement - showing us that the time has come. He is given a crown, for he is our King, for victory. This is his victory ride, his lap of honour - for this is the final victory.

"And he will destroy in this mountain the face of the covering

48

cast over all people, and the vail that is spread over all nations. He will swallow up death in victory ..." **(Isaiah 25:7-9)**

"For this corruptible must put on incorruption, and this mortal must put on immortality. So when this corruptible shall have put on incorruption, and this mortal shall have put on immortality, then shall be brought to pass the saying that is written, Death is swallowed up in victory" **(1 Corinthians 15:53-55)**

It is time for Jesus, with God the Father, to take control. Jesus 'went forth conquering' (opening the seals), breaking down the barriers between the mansions. As each is opened the corresponding colour disappears from his aura. The second seal symbolises warfare, the third famine, the fourth plague, the fifth religious persecution and the sixth Acts of God (natural disasters).

In Chapter 7, the vision goes on to remind us to assume that we are all descendants of the twelve tribes of Israel and that now is the time for everyone to progress towards the heavenly Jerusalem.

"Therefore are they before the throne of God, and serve him day and night in his temple: and he that sitteth on the throne shall dwell among them. They shall hunger no more, neither thirst any more; neither shall the sun light on them, nor any heat. For the Lamb which is in the midst of the throne shall feed them, and shall lead them unto living fountains of waters; and God shall wipe away all tears from their eyes." **(Revelation 5:15-17)**

The symbolic elite - those who have washed their robes white in the faith of Jesus Christ - are already in the heavenly Jerusalem, in their rightful place, along with the holy angels around the throne of God, waiting for Jesus.

In Chapter 8 we reach the climax of the unveiling as, through the vision, the divine mystery is fully revealed as Jesus opens the seventh and final seal of the violet ring into the heavenly Jerusalem..

"And when he had opened the seventh seal, there was silence in heaven about the space of half an hour." **(Revelation 8:1)**

This opens with what must be the most awesome of pregnant pauses and if we recall Peter and his philosophy of time *"... that one day is with the Lord as a thousand years, and a thousand years as one day."* - this silence may last for almost twenty-one years, such will be the impact! The earth and all its sinfulness no longer exist

49

and every spirit has returned to the spirit world. No longer can the truth be hidden; all that was detestable on earth has been conquered and swallowed up in the victory of Christ. All the restrictions of the many mansions have now been removed by the opening of the seals. I believe the message of this vision to be that, at the end of time, there will be no need for these restrictions to separate the many mansions. The vision tells us of our faults and the horrors of the world - "man's inhumanity to man" and shows us what is to be, in the spirit world. This is a potent message for today: man is destroying the earth, hurting his fellow man; so what is there to look forward to? Paradise in heaven! Having cast off all the colours, God and Jesus will rule from the heavenly Jerusalem, their glory (the colours of the spectrum soaked back into the celebrated great white light) illuminating the mansions - repelling all sin! It is only at this point that we will get the two extremes; those cast out to the red ring and those with the opportunity to progress, as far as they are able, towards the centre, the heavenly Jerusalem.

Isaiah illustrates this for us:

"I form the light, and create darkness: I make peace, and create evil: I the Lord do all these things." **(Isaiah 45:7)**

God's love is unconditional, accepts everyone for what they are - good or bad. In acknowledging that He has created all things, He now accepts responsibility for the two extremes. He even takes responsibility for those who are loathsome, those He has cast out. He could extinguish them but instead provides a place where they are made to suffer the torture of their own guilt.

Jesus says,

"When once the master of the house is risen up, and hath shut to the door, and ye begin to stand without, and to knock at the door, saying, Lord, Lord, open unto us; and he shall answer and say unto you, I know you not whence ye are: Then shall ye begin to say, We have eaten and drunk in thy presence, and thou hast taught in our street. But he shall say, I tell you, I know you not whence ye are; depart from me, all ye workers of iniquity. There shall be weeping and gnashing of teeth, when ye shall see Abraham and Isaac, and Jacob, and all the prophets, in the kingdom of God, and you yourselves thrust out. And they shall come from the east, and from

50

the west, and from the north, and from the south, and shall sit down in the kingdom of God." (**St Luke 13:25-30**)

Here, Jesus is talking about himself: having passed from the earth to the spirit world, he is now master of the heavenly Jerusalem. Many assume that because they have faith, attend church or take confession, they are favourites to enter the heavenly Jerusalem. They read and learn about Jesus, take the bread and wine (believing themselves to be in the presence of Jesus) and think that this gives automatic access to the heavenly Jerusalem. It is not enough to do these things. Jesus explains that they may have to remain outside, that they may not be worthy to progress as far as the centre. There is no preferential treatment for these people, it will all depend on how they have lived their lives!

James reminds us of this:

"Ye see then how that by works a man is justified, and not by faith only" (**James 2:24**)

"For as the body without the spirit is dead, so faith without works is dead also." (**James 2:26**)

If a man has deliberately turned his back on the light, by which he may have walked, he may find it difficult to face the light in a much clearer world. He may seek out the outer mansions, for a period of time, together with all those who need never have lost their way; those who, even without their bodies, find it hard to escape the fantasies of the mind and yet again postpone the desire for the glory of the vision of God.

51

Chapter 5
"A DOVE FLEW OVER GALILEE"

I believe that my spiritual gifts and experiences inspired me to read the Bible. They have definitely given me that extra insight into the gospel accounts of the life of Jesus, one of my favourite subjects, which I have now studied very carefully. Many of my findings are steeped in mystery; I have found evidence of the truth in the Bible and I now offer some explanation.

Let us look at the life of Jesus to discover what made him so different from ordinary men. Even though we know that he was an exceptional man, and that his qualities were faultless, we must never lose sight of the fact that he came to earth as a human being: a man in a physical body.

"And the Word was made flesh, and dwelt among us, (and we beheld his glory, the glory as of the only begotten of the Father,) full of grace and truth." **(St John 1:14)**

If it had not been so, then ordinary human beings could not be expected to follow his example, his teachings or to practice what he preached. As I have said before, he was a man of mystery, simply because he was without sin. When did any one of us ever embrace the company of such a person in the flesh? Jesus was one of the few human beings ever to attain that superior aura of righteousness while in the physical body. The only comparisons I can make are the spirits that I have been in contact with. They have already progressed, within the many mansions, to become more spiritually evolved.

Jesus lived with Joseph and Mary. As he grew in wisdom and strength, he worked in his father's shop. Jesus and his father were carpenters in Nazareth, a town in Galilee. He came to regenerate society, known as "the new dispensation". Being a carpenter by trade, he fashioned ploughs and yokes and these became symbolic in his teaching and ministry. The plough turns the soil, burying the old to bring the new into the light; it channels straight lines, so that crops can be planted to bring new life which the sower can harvest when ripe. The yoke is an instrument of burden crafted for use by a pair of draught animals, usually oxen, so that they can work together as a team and share the load, or a frame made to fit over a person's shoulders for carrying - either made to create harmony and balance. Jesus preached in parables, usually side by side, giving two examples, using familiar items such as the plough and yoke to illustrate his point.

"Come unto me, all ye that labour and are heavy laden, and I will give you rest. Take my yoke upon you, and learn of me: for I am meek and lowly in heart: and ye shall find rest unto your souls. For my yoke is easy, and my burden is light." **(St Matthew 11:28-end)**

Jesus dressed in ordinary clothes; he did not wear the soft purple linen of his contemporaries, nor sweeping robes as did the Levites, Scribes or Pharisees, nor any uniform denoting social status. His simple dress could not hide his purity, glowing like the reflection of the sun on a great lake. His gaze, incorporating the innocence of a child and embracing the wisdom of age, revealed his knowledge and love of nature.

Jesus had an average physique; he obviously had the strength in his arms and shoulders required for his manual work as a carpenter. He was pure in mind and body and because of his innate knowledge he was not burdened by everyday life. He was in a league of his own and this advantage manifested itself in his state of perfect health. He was not black or white; his skin was olive, a combination of the two. His eyes were not blue or brown but hazel, a cross between the two. As legend has it, his hair was a wine colour, not black or fair. He was Jewish and yet did not have that Jewish stereotyped look. God, in his wisdom and aware of human prejudice, created him so that he could not be identified with a particular race.

Jesus was 'on the road' for more than three years and he covered great distances. He travelled continuously from place to place, by day or night. He was at the service of all who called - lepers, cripples, the lame, deaf, dumb and blind. He apparently had no set itinerary and yet would sometimes insist on a particular route or could be diverted. The reasons always became clear. He always honoured the religious festivals and feast days; he made a point to attend these events.

His ministry lasted for three years, but the teachings of Jesus cannot be measured in human terms. This was a man whose words were inspired by the sensitivity of his spirit; he was in tune with the whole of God's creation. He preached about green fields, flowers, trees, the sky, sunrise and sunset, wind and rain, clouds and lightening, streams and rivers, stars and lamps, honey and salt. He spoke of bulrushes, burning weeds, wine, eggs, serpents, birds and animals, pearls and money, nets of fish, wheat, corn and oil, stewards and gardeners, farmers, labourers and employers, kings and shepherds, mother, fathers and families. Jesus knew all about life, especially human nature, and he used this knowledge to advocate a moral lifestyle. He knew the world before it began; he always was and always will be.

St. John tells us, that on entering the temple on one occasion Jesus drove out the sheep and the cattle and turned over the tables of the greedy dealers and money changers. He merely told the dove sellers to take their birds out of the temple; these were the doves sold to the poor for use as 'sin offering'. The gentleness of his nature would not allow him to hurt even the smallest of creatures, such as the doves.

He melted the hearts of those young fishermen with the words, "Come and see, follow me" as he offered for the first time that famous invitation, which is now open to all of mankind. He could look into people's auras, as he did when he saw Nathanael under the fig tree and said, "Here is a man with no guile." We are told that while Jesus was preaching in the temple, the crowd would often want to stone him or to take hold of him. He was able to disappear through the midst of them - was this by some divine intervention?

Jesus often played down his miracles, for fear that the people would put God in second place to these works. His love for God was pure and never impaired. He claimed no authority of his own, only the authority of his heavenly Father. He had a great knowledge of the scriptures, cushioned deep within his heart, he would quote Isaiah, Jeremiah, Daniel, Joel, Hosea, Micah, Zechariah, Malachi and the Psalms. There are no records of him studying with any of the great rabbis of the time. Jesus would often, however, disappear up to the mountains or into the garden and spend long periods of time alone; we are led to believe that it was at these times that he communed with God. His greatest works were done in his silence.

Jesus mixed at all levels of society with all types of people, especially sinners, the sick and children. His diet was simple, all things in moderation; even on feast days he never drank or ate to excess. He did not own any property or land or carry a purse; he had no possessions or worldly goods. His native language was Aramaic; he was a natural linguist and spoke many languages. Faced daily with Greek and Hebrew, he did not need an interpreter. Jesus fulfilled the law by perfectly keeping it.

Jesus held out his hand to calm the storms of everyday life. He walked the earth and on the sea. He washed the feet of his disciples and taught them of life and death. He spoke of Abraham, Moses, Jacob, David and Elijah. Jesus emptied himself of glory to live an earthly life; a life of mystery, sadness, hope and love. He was sold for thirty pieces of silver and crucified on a wooden cross. He rose on the third day so that we may live again in eternal life. Indeed, a dove flew over Galilee.

Let us now continue with some of the most precious accounts of important moments in the life of Jesus, where certain people were instantly able to recognise him as the Messiah:

"And when the days of her purification according to the law of Moses were accomplished they brought him to Jerusalem, to present him to the Lord; (As it is written in the law of the Lord, Every male that openeth the womb shall be called holy to the Lord;) And to offer a sacrifice according to the which is said in the law of the Lord, A pair of turtle doves, or two young pigeons. And, behold, there was a man in Jerusalem, whose name was Simeon; and the same man was just and devout, waiting for the consolation of Israel: and the Holy Ghost was upon him. And it was revealed unto him by the Holy Ghost, that he should not see death, before he had seen the Lord's Christ. And he came by the Spirit into the temple: and when the parents brought in the child Jesus, to do for him after the custom of the law, Then took he him up in his arms, and blessed God, and said, Lord, now lettest thou thy servant depart in peace, according to thy word: For mine eyes have seen thy salvation. Which thou hast prepared before the face of all people; a light to lighten the Gentiles, and the glory of thy people Israel." **(St Luke 2:22-33)**

Jesus was presented at the temple as a baby, in accordance

with the law and custom of the time: that every first born male is consecrated to the Lord. The proper offerings for such an occasion were a yearling lamb and a pigeon or turtle-dove. We are told that Mary and Joseph brought a pair of birds as a sacrifice - the traditional offering of the poor. Yet, here we have Mary and Joseph bringing the Lord of the Temple to the Temple of the Lord. They drew no attention to themselves and no-one could have suspected that this was the holy family. This incident is beautifully captured by St Luke and made memorable by the fact that Simeon recognises the Christ Child. We are told that Simeon was a devout Israelite, endowed with the gift of prophecy. Having received divine intimation that he would not die until he had seen the Messiah, he entered the temple on some inspired impulse. Recognising the holy child, he took him in his arms and burst into the glorious song, *Nunc Dimittis* - the song of Simeon, that ever since has been so dear to Christian hearts. The prophecy that the baby would be a light to the Gentiles was seven hundred years old:

"I the Lord have called thee in righteousness, and will hold thine hand, and will keep thee, and give thee for a covenant of the people, for a light of the Gentiles." **(Isaiah 42:6)**

Simeon recognises Jesus because he sees him shining like a pillar of light in his mother's arms; Simeon was seeing the aura of the holy child.

"And there was one Anna, a prophetess, the daughter of Phanuel, of the tribe of Aser: She was of a great age, and had lived with an husband seven years from her virginity; And she was a widow of about fourscore and four years, which departed not from the temple, but served God with fastings and prayers night and day. And she coming in that instant gave thanks likewise unto the Lord, and spoke of him to all them that looked for redemption in Jerusalem." **(St Luke 2:36-39)**

Anna, like Mary, would have been betrothed at a very early age, possibly while still in her teens, and her husband may have been a lot older. They were married for only seven years. She was now a grand old widow of eighty-four and never left the temple, serving God night and day. Her age and her environment must have affected her eyesight. The temple was a dark and dingy place, dimly lit only by a torch which was kept constantly burning above the altar. Yet she was still able to see something special about the baby Jesus, and she must have seen hundreds of firstborn males presented at the temple. We are told that Anna was a prophetess, so she too was endowed with spiritual gifts. She saw for herself what Simeon had seen: the aura of the Holy Child.

The Transfiguration is of great spiritual importance as we study the life of Jesus in terms of how others saw him. 'Transfiguration' is defined as the change in the appearance of Christ that took place before three disciples, in the following account from Luke:

"Now about eight days after this had been said, he took with him Peter, John and James and went up the mountain to pray. And it happened that, as he was praying, the aspect of his face was changed and his clothing became sparkling white. And suddenly there were two men talking to him, they were Moses and Elijah appearing in glory, and they were speaking of his passing which he was to accomplish in Jerusalem. Peter and his companions were heavy with sleep, but they woke up and saw his glory and the two men standing with him. As these were leaving him, Peter said to Jesus, 'Master, it is wonderful for us to be here; so let us make three shelters, one for you, one for Moses and one for Elijah.' He did not know what he was saying. As he was saying this, a cloud came and covered them with shadow; and when they went into the cloud the disciples were afraid. And a voice came from the cloud saying, 'This is my Son, the Chosen One. Listen to him.' And after the voice had spoken, Jesus was found alone. The disciples kept silence and, at that time, told no one what they had seen." **(St Luke 9:28-37)**

The Transfiguration, this momentous occasion in the life of Jesus, followed a conversation between Jesus and the disciples about his death. He then took the three main disciples: John, James and Peter, up to the mountain with him. These three were the most enlightened of the group and the closest and dearest to him. This event did not happen by chance, but was part of a divine plan. Jesus was inspired to go up to the mountain; we are not told the details.

The Transfiguration had to happen. There, he knelt and prayed, to the point of ecstasy. As he prayed, he was elevated far above the everyday life of the world and far above those who had rejected him. He was now in a state of deep meditation, his spirit flowing out along his silver cord - his direct prayer line to his heavenly Father, who was now to bring about, upon that mountain, a transfiguration of great importance. He was by this time 'out of the body' (i.e. in the spirit), in all his glory. Jesus was now transfigured before his disciples; his whole being shone like the sun and his clothing as white as the dazzling snowfields above them. He was bathed in an aura of brilliance and radiance. His appearance changed so, because he was 'out of the body'. Then, two figures appeared by his side: Moses and Elijah. As they were also 'in the spirit' they came in a blaze of glory. Their power, added to the magnificence of Jesus Christ, must have produced a brilliant light, like a searchlight or floodlight dominating the landscape. By now, night had fallen on the mountain; this must have been some sight as the darkness was engulfed and the scenery swallowed up by the light. As I have already said, I have witnessed such light - when my guardian angel appeared to me. Jesus became part of an overpowering spiritual light; the Transfiguration was actually his transition from the physical to the spiritual. The fact that he was 'out of the body' accounted for the Transfiguration. The three of them spoke of the impending death of Jesus; the disciples woke to witness this sight.

Elijah was the great prophet who was taken up to heaven in a horse drawn chariot of fire:

"And it came to pass, as they still went on, and talked, that, behold, there appeared a chariot of fire, and horses of fire, and parted them both asunder; and Elijah went up by a whirlwind into heaven."
(2 Kings 2:11)

This phenomenon is known as 'being taken without seeing corruption'. Enoch, another prophet, who lived between the time of Adam and the Great Flood, was also taken without seeing corruption:
"And Enoch walked with God: and he was not; for God took him."
(Genesis 5:24)

Elijah had passed hundreds of years before the Transfiguration; he lived around eight hundred and fifty years before

Christ. According to traditional Christian beliefs, Elijah came to represent the prophets at the Transfiguration. The true and more spiritual reason for his presence in the spirit at the Transfiguration is that he was the best example of one 'taken without seeing corruption'; he did not experience death on earth, but was taken at the end of his life on earth.

Moses had the reputation of a great lawgiver; he was the prophet who led the first great exodus towards the promised land. He lived twelve hundred and fifty years before Christ. According to traditional Christian beliefs, Moses came to represent the law at the Transfiguration.

"So Moses the servant of the Lord died there in the land of Moab, according to the word of the Lord. And he buried him in a valley in the land of Moab, over against Bethpeor: but no man knoweth of his sepulchre unto this day." **(Deuteronomy 34:5-7)**

Moses appeared at the Transfiguration as the example of one who had died and been buried but whose body had never been found.

Some Christian groups believe that all the prophets are still waiting, in their graves, for the last trumpet when they will be re-formed from the earth.

The Transfiguration was the preparation ground for Jesus, leading to his death and burial. Elijah and Moses, by appearing at the Transfiguration, were paving the way for their attendance at the sepulchre of Jesus Christ. This tied in with the truth: that Jesus was to die, be buried, resurrected and raised up, on the third day, without seeing corruption. This was to be the way for Jesus: a combination of the experiences of the two prophets, Elijah and Moses. It was not a coincidence that the Transfiguration took place in the way that it did; it was for the benefit of the three most important disciples - for them to witness the three men together: Jesus, the perfect man, and the two highly-evolved spirits of Elijah and Moses, to hear the voice of God, to strengthen their faith for Calvary.

We are told that the disciples told no-one of what they had seen. Jesus had probably warned them at the time not to speak of this event. They had seen Elijah and Moses, seen Jesus 'out of the body' and heard the voice of God. They had been given the proof by God, the Father, that Jesus was His Son and of life after death!

The dictionary defines 'soul' as the spirit or immaterial part of man, the seat of human personality, intellect, will and emotions, regarded as an entity that survives the body after death. Let us now look at the story of the widow's son, in which God helps Elijah to return the soul of the boy and bring him back to life:

"It happened after this that the son of the mistress of the house fell sick, his illness was so severe that in the end he expired. And the woman said to Elijah, 'What quarrel have you with me, man of God? Have you come here to bring my sins home to me and to kill my son?' 'Give me your son,' he said and, taking him from her lap, he carried him to the upper room where he was staying and laid him on his bed. He cried out to Yahweh, 'Yahweh my God, do you mean to bring grief even to the widow who is looking after me by killing her son?' He stretched himself on the child three times and cried out to Yahweh, 'Yahweh my God, may the soul of this child, I beg you, come into him again!' Yahweh heard Elijah's prayer and the child's soul came back into his body and he revived. Elijah took the child, brought him down from the upper room into the house, and gave him to his mother. 'Look', Elijah said, 'your son is alive.' And the woman replied, 'Now I know you are a man of God and the word of Yahweh in your mouth is truth itself.' " **(1 Kings 17:17-end)**

We now see the use of the word 'soul' rather than 'spirit', which is the term that I am more comfortable with; to my mind both words mean the same.

We are told that the boy is dead and that his soul has left his body. Elijah prays aloud to God (as a faithful prophet of the time would have been expected to do). He asks God to use him as an instrument to bring the soul of the boy back into his body. Elijah stretches himself on the child three times. This could only have been done by someone like Elijah, someone with a very powerful aura. God taps into that power, into the spiritual rather than the physical side of Elijah, and is able to work through that spirit, as they are of the same vibration. So here we have the Holy Spirit working through the spirit of a man. As he stretches himself on the boy, Elijah acts as the conductor of the power of God. He is the go-between for God to fuse the spiritual cord back into the boy's body. Elijah also acts as a filter, to dilute this great power, to protect the boy against the shock of the violent jolts caused by the soul re-entering the body, so that the boy suffers no ill effects.

This was not just an act of faith and Elijah could not have done this on his own; his prayers and faith alone would not have been enough. There had to be contact between himself and the boy and so he physically had to remove the boy up to his room onto his own bed for this to work. The cord had been severed; Elijah needed God's intervention to achieve the reconnection of the soul, to bring the boy back to life.

A sanctuary is a holy place, consecrated shrine or place of refuge. Throughout the Old Testament God requests from the people of Israel the construction of a sanctuary, i.e. temple, and this is achieved through Moses. This dwelling place of God becomes flesh as the sanctuary is personified by Jesus Christ:

"And David my servant shall be king over them; and they all shall have one shepherd: they shall also walk in my judgements, and observe my statutes, and do them. And they shall dwell in the land that I have given unto Jacob my servant, wherein your fathers have dwelt; and they shall dwell therein, even they, and their children, and their children's children for ever: and my servant David shall be their prince for ever. Moreover I will make a covenant of peace with them; it shall be an everlasting covenant with them: and I will place them, and multiply them, and will set my sanctuary in the midst of them for evermore." **(Ezekiel 37:24-27)**

Here we have Ezekiel telling us of God's intentions, looking six hundred years into the future. David, the servant, is the young shepherd boy, son of Jesse, later chosen to be King of Israel. Jesus is to be born through this princely line of David, to be the shepherd for all of mankind. Jesus will be a permanent sanctuary, where all may take refuge. This is God's everlasting covenant with man.

Jesus often refers to his own body as a temple; I find this an intriguing description which, through investigation, will lead us to the Crucifixion at Calvary. As with sanctuary, a temple is a place or object regarded as a shrine where God makes himself present.

61

"Jesus answered and said unto them, Destroy this temple, and in three days I will raise it up. Then said the Jews, Forty and six years was this temple in building and wilt thou rear it up in three days? But he spake of the temple of his body." (**St John 2:19-22**)

Jesus describes himself as a temple, in which he submits to the Father's will for evermore; this epitomises the authority of God and the submissiveness of Jesus.

As Jesus hung dying on the cross, between two common criminals, we hear a very important conversation:

"And one of the malefactors which were hanged railed on him, saying, If thou be Christ, save thyself and us. But the other answering rebuked him, saying, Dost not thou fear God, seeing thou art in the same condemnation? And we indeed justly; for we receive the due reward of our deeds: but this man hath done nothing amiss. And he said unto Jesus, Lord, remember me when thou comest into thy kingdom. And Jesus said unto him, Verily I say unto thee, To day shalt thou be with me in paradise." (**St Luke 23:39-44**).

The two thieves begin to judge themselves. The first follows the soldiers in ridiculing Jesus, hinting that if he was who he said he was, he could save himself and them. He has a very selfish attitude - wanting the easy option; he reveals the darker side of human nature and thus condemns himself.

The second rebukes the first, he knows that it is right and fitting that they are punished. In confessing his guilt, he admits that they deserve to die for what they have done - but that Jesus has done nothing wrong. He accepts his fate and asks to be remembered - for Jesus not to give up on him - in the kingdom to come. As with Jesus, he does not curse his accusers as he has the courage to judge himself. He has started his progression while still on the cross, lifting his spirit to a higher level.

Jesus does not forgive these men, neither does he condemn them. He realises that the second man has acknowledged the truth and has already started his progression; to give him comfort, he explains what is to be:

"To day shalt thou be with me in paradise." (**St Luke 23:43**)

This is his message to the world; he came to prove that there is eternal life for all - even for the common thief!

This man must have been a comfort to Jesus, in that he acknowledges the existence of the kingdom to come - the new law of mercy had been received and accepted.

That which Jesus promises in his humility, he will fulfil in his glory.

Let us now turn to St Paul who talks of his experience of paradise:

"I knew a man in Christ above fourteen years ago, (whether in the body, I cannot tell; or whether out of the body, I cannot tell: God knoweth) such an one caught up to the third heaven. And I knew such a man, (whether in the body, or out of the body, I cannot tell: God knoweth) How that he was caught up into paradise, and heard unspeakable words, which it is not lawful for a man to utter."
(2 Corinthians 12:2-5)

Here, St Paul is talking about one of his many out-of-body experiences. It must have been an overwhelming experience, as he still questions whether he had been in or out of the body. He realises that he was out of the body as he describes being taken to the third heaven. According to my calculation, this third heaven (as opposed to the first or second heaven) must be the blue ring of the rainbow mansions, a part of paradise. I have studied the life and works of St Paul and the blue ring would seem to be an accurate position within the many mansions for Paul at this time. This would have been his point of progression and at that stage in his life he would not have been allowed any higher. He was by this time a Christian, having experienced his famous vision and conversion on the road to Damascus. He had always been a devout man of God, having studied the Torah and religious law all his life. As a result of this, earlier in his life he had been given the authority to persecute the early Christians: he committed them to prison and even held the cloaks of those who stoned Stephen. We are not told who spoke to Paul in this third heaven; the words and knowledge were for Paul alone and forbidden to be repeated. He may have been in the presence of one of the great prophets, as I was when I had such an experience; I met Abdullah (not his real name) and was told things that I am not allowed to repeat.

The term paradise used here by Paul, and by Jesus to the thief on the cross, covers all the mansions - not just the top mansion at the centre.

Let us return to Luke's account of Jesus on the cross:

"And it was about the sixth hour, and there was a darkness over all the earth until the ninth hour. And the sun was darkened, and the veil of the temple was rent in the midst. And when Jesus had cried with a loud voice, he said, Father, into thy hands I commend my spirit: and having said thus, he gave up the ghost. Now when the centurion saw what was done, he glorified God, saying, Certainly this was a righteous man." **(St Luke 23:44-8)**

Here the sanctuary/temple of Jesus Christ is finally delivered to its spiritual glory. Jesus is the temple and the veil is his aura. Luke, as in other accounts, uses the symbolism of the elements. At the foot of the cross is the centurion, who would have been the officer in charge of the crucifixion. As he observes the proceedings, he concentrates on the differing emotions of all that is going on around him. He watches as the life drains out of Jesus and the light starts to fade; at his death, he makes his profound statement, "Certainly this was a righteous man". It is no sudden impulse that draws the centurion into a deeper understanding of the situation - he sees what others cannot see. At the death he sees what he failed to see before. It is what he is now not seeing that prompts him to say that Jesus was a righteous man; in other accounts he goes on to say that he was the son of God. He sees that the aura of Jesus Christ has been extinguished.

Imagine the brightest summer's day in the park or at the beach, and the sun has been shining nonstop all day. Suddenly a single cloud blocks out the sun for a few moments. The instant reaction is to change position and look up into the sky; that which we had taken for granted has now disappeared and it is only now that we realise how brightly the sun had been shining in the clear sky; a single cloud having the power to draw the gaze of many people.

It was the custom of the Roman soldiers to break the legs of those who were lingering death. The crucifixion was designed to be a slow death of suffocation. After a few hours the body would droop further and further until the torso was stretched; breathing would become difficult as the lungs became congested and full of fluid. When the legs were broken, the body would lose all support and breathing would become impossible. Jesus did not have his legs broken; when the soldiers came, he was already dead. This was the fulfilment of the scriptures:

"For these things were done, that the scripture should be fulfilled, A bone of him shall not be broken." **(St John 19:36)**

"But when they came to Jesus, and saw that he was dead already, they brake not his legs: But one of the soldiers with a spear pierced his side, and forthwith came there out blood and water." **(St John 19:33-35)**

One of the soldiers, in order to make sure that Jesus was dead, pierced his side with a spear. He who came by blood and water now suffered the final blow of the spear and as John emphatically tells us, "... forthwith came there out blood and water".

St John speaks of himself, as he was a witness at the Crucifixion, in the next verse:

"And he that saw it bare record, and his record is true: and he knoweth that he saith true, that ye might believe." **(St John 19:35)**

It is John who tells us of the manner of the birth of Jesus, i.e. a normal, physical birth:

"This is he that came by water and blood, even Jesus Christ; not by water only, but by water and blood." **(1 John 5:6)**

Now we have John emphasising the point that Jesus, as he came in human form, endured cruelty and humiliation in the flesh on the cross and suffered this death as a physical man.

It is also John who tells us about the famous conversation between Jesus and Nicodemus - about being 'born again' (which I have already explained in great detail). Nicodemus was present at the Crucifixion:

"And there came also Nicodemus, which at the first came to Jesus by night, and brought a mixture of myrrh and aloes, about an hundred pound weight. Then took they the body of Jesus, and wound it in linen clothes with the spices, as the manner of the Jews is to bury." **(St John 19:39-41)**

Nicodemus appears again to witness the death of Jesus, i.e.

the beginning of the process of his second birth, which was the lesson Jesus gave to Nicodemus at their first meeting long ago. Nicodemus, together with Joseph of Arimathea, now well aware that Jesus is the Messiah, has come to give him the burial of a king: with expensive linen, a large quantity of spices and a fresh tomb (sepulchre), belonging to Joseph of Arimathea.

For John, the centurion is a turning point in his discipleship. *"And again another scripture saith, They shall look on him whom they pierced."* (**St John 19:37**)

This represents the gentiles who were to be converted; many more looked up to him after the light had been extinguished. This now includes all nations; we are all to inherit eternal life!

We now come to the miracle of miracles - the Resurrection. Many alternative versions have been given, analysing the subject of the Resurrection, ranging from myth to masquerade. I am going to use the words of Jesus himself and the account St John gives us - because he was an eyewitness he can give us an hour by hour report. He gives us the actual facts in the correct order and so without adding or taking anything away, I can use St John to tell what really happened. I am able to interpret St John; I can relate to him; I understand and trust his account as being accurate. It is because of the insight gained from my experiences and spiritual gifts that I am able to glean the truth from John.

The whole of the life and ministry of Jesus Christ - his miracles, parables, teachings and sufferings - culminate in the Resurrection, the last and greatest miracle.

Jesus, all through his life, points us to his death and Resurrection; he prepares the disciples through proverbs. I will explain how it was done and that it did happen in the way that he said it would happen. Only Jesus knew what was to happen and it was for him alone to give that message to the world: that he would resurrect. The disciples did not fully understand until after his death and the scriptures were fulfilled.

Up until the Resurrection, Jesus, for many, was just another prophet; it was the Resurrection that made all the difference, in that it proved that he was the Son of God. Even now, Christian faith hinges on the Resurrection, without knowing the truth of it.

The truth of the Resurrection holds the key for us all. The purpose of it is to prove eternal life for all, from the poorest shepherd to the wealthiest king, from the most evil criminal to the saint. Jesus had to meet death in order to resurrect and only in this can Christians find the truth. We have failed, as a human race, to follow his example and to see the truth. The Resurrection is his message to the world. Through the Resurrection Jesus gives the message using the dual-purpose body for the last time - to finally give his message that eternal life is for all.

The star attending his birth - visible only to the chosen - led them to the stable. He, who was denied a room at the inn, now offers everyone a place in his Father's house. The many mansions, illuminated by the magnificent glory of God, now prepare for his return.

Jesus was the final solution, part of the great plan that God had made at the outset. In this divine plan He created everything to function in opposites, in pairs such as physical body and spiritual body, night and day, man and woman, hot and cold, good and evil, etc. Everything has an opposite. God is the Spirit, living in the spirit world; the final, and greatest, part of His plan was to send Jesus to earth, to experience a physical life in a physical body. As I have mentioned before, that which cannot be achieved on earth will be achieved in heaven; the failings of mankind on earth will be turned into success in the many mansions. By creating everything in opposites God cannot fail; only man falls short of the mark (the Hebrew for sin means missing the mark).

Jesus says:

"Destroy this temple, and in three days I will raise it up" **(St John 2:19)**

His body, placed in the sepulchre of Joseph of Arimathea, sustained three days of divine purification - the resulting body being 'incorruptible'. This is the body, the physical body, conceived of God, which like the spirit, belongs to God and is soon to return to God.

"The first day of the week cometh Mary Magdalene early, when it was yet dark, unto the sepulchre, and seeth the stone taken away from the sepulchre. Then she runneth, and cometh to Simon

Peter, and to the other disciple, whom Jesus loved, and saith unto them, They have taken away the Lord out of the sepulchre, and we know not where they have laid him. Peter therefore went forth, and that other disciple, and came to the sepulchre. So they ran both together: and the other disciple did outrun Peter, and came first to the sepulchre. And he stooping down, and looking in, saw the linen clothes lying; yet went he not in. Then cometh Simon Peter following him, and went into the sepulchre, and seeth the linen clothes lie, And the napkin, that was about his head, not lying with the linen clothes, but wrapped together in a place by itself. Then went in also that other disciple, which came first to the sepulchre, and he saw, and believed. For as yet they knew not the scripture, that he must rise again from the dead. Then the disciples went away again unto their own home. But Mary stood without at the sepulchre weeping: and as she wept, she stooped down, and looked into the sepulchre, And seeth two angels in white sitting, the one at the head, and the other at the feet, where the body of Jesus had lain. And they say unto her, Woman, why weepest thou? She saith unto them Because they have taken away my Lord, and I know not where they have laid him. And when she had thus said, she turned herself back, and saw Jesus standing, and knew not that it was Jesus. Jesus saith unto her Woman, why weepest thou? whom seekest thou? She supposing him to be the gardener saith unto him, Sir, if thou have borne him hence, tell me where thou hast laid him, and I will take him away. Jesus saith unto her, Mary. She turned herself, and saith unto him, Rabboni, which is to say, Master. Jesus saith unto her, Touch me not; for I am not yet ascended to my Father: but go to my brethren, and say unto them, I ascend unto my Father, and your Father; and to my God, and your God." **(St John 20:1-18)**

The "stone taken away from the sepulchre" is a very important part of this commentary. Much has been written over the years about the stone being moved, omitting the reason for this. The spirit has re-entered the body, after the purification process, bringing back the life force and Jesus now appears in his physical body. The removal of the stone is our first clue in proving this. We have already established that only spirits can pass through matter. If, as many believe, Jesus is in the spirit at this time, there would be no reason for the removal of the stone. Imagine the alternative: that Jesus is in the spirit and passes through the sepulchre wall. When Mary Magdalene and the disciples reach the tomb they find Jesus sitting on a nearby rock. They order the stone to be rolled away to find the body gone - has it miraculously evaporated or dematerialised? No, Jesus resurrects in the physical body. I believe that the stone was removed, by divine intervention, to prove that Jesus returned in his physical body. He could not have removed the stone himself. He would have been contaminated; his body had to remain 'incorruptible'. Why would he now complicate his simple teaching by resurrecting as a spirit?

Mary sees what John describes as "two angels in white sitting, the one at the head, and the other at the feet, where the body of Jesus had lain." The disciples, Peter and John, on looking into the tomb, see only the burial robes. These were two of the most enlightened of the apostolic band; the awesome sight of the Transfiguration was for their benefit. On her own admission Mary sees the two angels; these were the same two who attended Jesus at the Transfiguration: Elijah and Moses. Mary, with an impassioned soul, is painfully suffering the anguish of discovering her master's body gone; not even Elijah and Moses can pacify her. In her torment, her whole being absorbed in the puzzle of the missing body, she fails to recognize them. She turns and sees a man; she does not recognise Jesus at first, believing him to be a mere gardener. Here we have the second clue that Jesus is in the physical body. In the spirit he would have been a most spectacular sight. As Jesus speaks her name, she is jolted back into reality. Mary proclaims him "Rabboni", which means 'Master' She reaches out to touch him and Jesus says, "Touch me not; for I am not yet ascended to my Father."

Here he gives us the third clue that he is in the physical body. Unlike the woman who reached out and touched the hem of his garment and instantly gained her desire, he is denying Mary Magdalene, one of his most faithful followers, her request. The very touch of Mary Magdalene would have undone the whole purification process, so she must not touch him. His purpose, now, was to ascend to his heavenly Father without seeing corruption, in a pure, physical body. In the same way that he walked on (above) water, he is now levitated, slightly above the ground, in order to avoid being 'corrupted'. This is the man who physically touched, and was touched by, everyone, including those polluted, if not by sin, by their infirmities; he did not refuse even the most detestable of outcasts, the lepers. Remember here the words of Paul, "For this corruptible must put on incorruption, and this mortal must put on immortality." Many people believe that when Jesus spoke the famous words "Touch me not ..." he was telling Mary Magdalene not to cling to him, thus breaking down their personal relationship. If Mary had looked deeper into these prophetic words of Jesus, she could have understood his meaning.

The presence of Elijah and Moses in the tomb is significant: the great Elijah, who brought the widow's son back to life, and the great Moses, who led the first exodus to the promised land. Together, Elijah and Moses spoke to Jesus, at the Transfiguration, about his death. Here they are to oversee and witness all that they spoke about at the Transfiguration, i.e. the Resurrection in the physical body, and the fulfilment of the scriptures to the last detail - bringing the Old and New Testaments together.

Jesus said to the disciples, Peter, John and James, as they came down the mountain after the Transfiguration:

"Tell the vision to no man, until the Son of Man be risen again from the dead. And his disciples asked him, saying, Why then say the scribes that Elias [=Elijah] *must first come? And Jesus answered and said unto them, Elias* [=Elijah] *truly shall first come, and restore all things."* **(Matthew 17:9-12)**

This is Christ's message referring to Elijah, one of the greatest men of all time, and his presence in the tomb, telling us that this highly-evolved spirit is to be a party to the purification process, as his very presence will repel any contamination. He is to protect and then restore the body of Christ to ensure that this is no ordinary death - but the miracle of miracles. Jesus is 'all things': the light and the way, the Alpha and the Omega.

All the laws and commandments that were given to Moses by God to pass on to the Israelites - the chosen people - are finally (and only) completed through Jesus Christ. Jesus, in the way he lived his life, perfectly kept these laws. It is therefore fitting for Moses to be present in the tomb and to be a party to the Resurrection. Together with Moses, Jesus will now lead us all to the final promised land.

70

The Resurrection of Jesus Christ was a physical one (as the gospels confirm) - albeit for only a few hours. If this had been a spiritual Resurrection we need to know what happened to the body!

Jesus brought others back to life. Lazarus had been dead for four days; Jesus called him out of his tomb. Jesus said, *"I am the resurrection ..."* (**St John 11:25**). At a command from Jesus, the daughter of Jairus was brought back to life; as was the son of the widow of Nain, who woke from the dead, sat up and began to talk.

A spiritual resurrection would have meant that Jesus was just an ordinary human being, with an earthly father - giving him the same experience at death that we all have. His parentage was crucial to his Resurrection, proving that he was the Son of God, enabling his whole being, both physical and spiritual, to ascend to his Father:

"And this is the Father's will which hath sent me, that of all which he hath given me I should lose nothing, but should raise it up again at the last day." (**St John 6:39**)

The last words of Jesus, in the physical body, to Mary Magdalene, are:

"... go to my brethren, and say unto them, I ascend unto my Father, and your Father; and to my God, and your God." (**St John 20:17**)

He gives, through Mary Magdalene, his message to the world; now is the time for him to enter into his glory. This does not point to the Ascension after forty days, but to the present. If the Ascension was to be after forty days, why would Jesus use such language? He says, "I ascend ...", meaning there and then, on the same day as the Resurrection. There is no mystery, therefore, regarding his body.

In life, Jesus refers to himself as do the scriptures, as the Son of Man - a fitting title for the Son of God in a physical body. Now, after the Resurrection, at the Ascension, Jesus truly is the glorified Son of God.

It was still early in the morning when Jesus spoke to Mary Magdalene. Later that same day, at some time during the afternoon, two disciples were on their way to Emmaus, a village seven miles from Jerusalem, when they were joined by Jesus whom they did not recognise at first. I refer here to St Luke, as St John makes no

71

reference to the Emmaus road:

"And, behold, two of them went that same day to a village called Emmaus, which was from Jerusalem about three score furlongs. And they talked together of all these things which had happened. And it came to pass, that, while they communed together and reasoned, Jesus himself drew near, and went with them. But their eyes were holden that they should not know him. And he said unto them, What manner of communications are these that ye have one to another, as ye walk, and are sad? And the one of them, whose name was Cleopas, answering said unto him, Art thou only a stranger in Jerusalem, and hast not known the things which are come to pass there in these days? And he said unto them, What things? And they said unto him, Concerning Jesus of Nazareth, which was a prophet mighty in deed and word before God and all the people: And how the chief priests and our rulers delivered him to be condemned to death, and have crucified him. But we trusted that it had been he which should have redeemed Israel: and beside all this, to day is the third day since these things were done. Yea, and certain women also of our company made us astonished, which were early at the sepulchre; And when they found not his body, they came, saying, that they had also seen a vision of angels, which said that he was alive. And certain of them which were with us went to the sepulchre, and found it even so as the women had said but him they saw not. Then he said unto them, O fools, and slow of heart to believe all that the prophets have spoken! Ought not Christ to have suffered these things, and to enter into his glory? And beginning at Moses and all the prophets, he expounded unto them in all the Scriptures the things concerning himself. And they drew nigh unto the village, whither they went: and he made as though he would have gone further. But they constrained him, saying, Abide with us: for it is toward evening, and the day is far spent. And he went in to tarry with them. And it came to pass, as he sat at meat with them, he took bread, and blessed it, and brake, and gave to them. And their eyes were opened, and they knew him; and he vanished out of their sight. And they said one to another, Did not our heart burn within us, while he talked with us by the way, and while he opened to us the Scriptures?" **(St Luke 24:13-33)**

Within a few hours Jesus ascends to the Father and now

returns as a fully-materialised spirit. He has shed his body and emerges like a butterfly from its cocoon - all the preparation for this having been done during those three days after his death, as the bodies separated: the spirit body having returned to the many mansions and the physical body purified in the tomb under the supervision of Elijah and Moses.

I refer to this account from Luke as it proves that Jesus has returned 'in the spirit'. If he were not a spirit how could he appear on the Emmaus road, not as an invalid with terrible wounds in need of nursing back to health, but as a man fit enough to walk the seven miles to Emmaus? A man would not have been able to walk with such wounds.

The language of this piece gives it away that he returns 'in the spirit'. In verse 15 we are told that "Jesus himself drew near"; "drew near" meaning materialised, proving that he appears to the disciples 'in the spirit'. He comes to explain to them what the prophets had written about him in the scriptures. This will all have been accurate as it comes from the lips of Jesus Christ himself. They are overjoyed to hear these scriptures exactly as the prophets had written them and yet now feel somewhat guilty as earlier in their discussions they had expressed sadness and disappointment. Even though they regarded Jesus as a powerful prophet - in both action and words - they were wondering, in their own minds, if he had been just another prophet; he had not set Israel free as they had hoped and they were now feeling 'let down'. They were questioning also the fact that he was condemned to death and crucified, i.e. that he experienced death as an ordinary man.

The disciples do not recognise Jesus, as a spirit there must have been something very different in his appearance. As he explains the scriptures, they begin to understand and to realise the truth. He speaks to them in such a way that they remember his life and that he had lived exactly as the scriptures had predicted. After all their doubts and misgivings these disciples are now able to make the connection.

At table, Jesus blesses and breaks the bread, and gives it to the two disciples. With this, they recognise Jesus. It had been the custom during his lifetime for Jesus, and only Jesus, to give the blessing before breaking the bread; this happened at any gathering, for example, the last supper, the miracle of the loaves and any meeting of the disciples. They now realise that Jesus is the Son of God and that they are in the presence of the risen Christ.

Jesus appears to these lesser-known disciples in order to ensure that he proves this point at all levels, for them to witness he has risen, i.e. ascended, on the third day. It would be deemed biased for him to appear only to his own 'elite' group.

At this point of recognition, Jesus 'vanishes' - giving us absolute proof that he is 'in the spirit' at this time; physical bodies cannot vanish! Jesus does not allow for any discussion at this point.

In verse 26 of Luke's account Jesus says:

"Ought not Christ to have suffered these things, and to enter into his glory?" **(St Luke 24:26)**

He tells the disciples of his life, through the scriptures, before entering into his glory, i.e. before his ascension. He is telling us that he has, in fact, already ascended.

Jesus appears to the disciples that same evening:

"Then the same day at evening, being the first day of the week, when the doors were shut where the disciples were assembled for fear of the Jews, came Jesus and stood in the midst, and saith unto them, Peace be unto you. And when he had so said, he shewed unto them his hands and his side. Then were the disciples glad, when they saw the Lord." **(St John 20:19-21)**

John tells us that the disciples are gathered together (and John is one of them) with the doors shut. The doors are locked and well secured as the disciples are in fear for their lives at the hands of the Jews.

Mary Magdalene has reported back to them, by this time:

"Mary Magdalene came and told the disciples that she had seen the Lord, and that he had spoken these things unto her." **(St John 20:18)**

They are also aware, by this time, of the appearance of Christ on the Emmaus road. John does not tell us about Emmaus (he only tells us of the things that he, himself, has witnessed).

"And they rose up the same hour, and returned to Jerusalem, and found the eleven gathered together, and them that were with

them, Saying, The Lord is risen indeed, and hath appeared to Simon.
And they told what things were done in the way, and how he was
known of them in breaking of bread." **(St Luke 24:33-36)**

The disciples now know from these witnesses that the
Resurrection and the Ascension have been achieved on that same day
- the third day!

As they are talking together, Jesus comes and stands in the
midst of them. The language used by John suggests that Jesus either
materialises before them or passes through the wall to appear in front
of them 'in the spirit'. Full materialisations can, according to the
atmosphere, take just a few seconds or may take a few minutes. I
suggest that in this case Jesus materialises before them and that this
takes a few minutes.

The atmosphere in this room is highly charged; the disciples
saddened by the death of Jesus, in shock after hearing about the
empty tomb and sightings of Jesus and fearful as they hide from the
Jews. They are traumatised and mystified by the events of the last
few days. They wonder why Jesus offered no resistance and why
no-one defended him or delivered him from such a terrible death.
They feel guilty and cowardly as they did not help him. One had
betrayed him and one had denied him and all had scattered at the
garden of Gethsemane at the time of his arrest. Even the elements
objected as a storm raged; at midday, the time of the death, the sun
darkened and the earth quaked. The disciples assumed some divine
intervention at this point and that Jesus would be saved - but nothing
was forthcoming!

The conditions in the room, therefore, are hardly conducive
to the acceptance of a spirit. To calm the situation and to allay their
fears, Jesus appears to the disciples very slowly and gently with the
wonderful greeting, "Shalom Aleichem", which means in Hebrew,
'Peace be with you'. To reassure them, Jesus shows them his hands
and his side, for recognition. A materialisation can take any form or
shape. There is nothing extraordinary in the fact that Jesus appears
to them in the way that they last saw him, i.e. with the wounds he
suffered on the cross. As we have already established, spirits have to
appear to us as we knew them, for recognition. In the case of Jesus,
he has to appear fully materialised, showing his wounds, to give

absolute proof that it really is him. As soon as the disciples realise that this is Jesus 'in the spirit' they are joyful (as Jesus had foretold):

"Verily, verily, I say unto you, That ye shall weep and lament, but the world shall rejoice: and ye shall be sorrowful, but your sorrow shall be turned into joy." **(St John 16:20)**

Thomas is not with the other disciples when Jesus appears to them, but they report back to him:

"We have seen the Lord. But he said unto them, Except I shall see in his hands the print of the nails, and put my finger into the print of the nails, and thrust my hand into his side, I will not believe." **(St John 20:25-6)**

For this, Thomas has come to be known as 'doubting Thomas'. Unless he sees for himself he will not believe. He is given proof a short while later:

"And after eight days again his disciples were within, and Thomas with them: then came Jesus, the doors being shut, and stood in the midst, and said, Peace be unto you. Then saith he to Thomas, Reach hither thy finger, and behold my hands; and reach hither thy hand, and thrust it into my side: and be not faithless, but believing. And Thomas answered and said unto him, My Lord and my God. Jesus saith unto him, Thomas, because thou hast seen me, thou hast believed: blessed are they that have not seen, and yet have believed." **(St John 20:26-30)**

Here, Jesus appears to the disciples once more - this time for the benefit of Thomas. Again the doors are locked, telling us that Jesus comes 'in the spirit', once more in a recognisable form, showing his wounds. By reiterating the concerns of Thomas, Jesus invites his touch, giving him the opportunity to put his hands into these wounds. Mary Magdalene had not been allowed to touch Jesus. Now, Jesus is positively encouraging investigation; his spirit body cannot be contaminated by contact with human hands. We do not know if Thomas takes up this offer - there is now no need; it is enough for him to see, to believe. Thomas now humbly acknowledges Jesus as 'My Lord and my God'. In life he would have addressed Jesus as Lord or Master; he is now seeing Jesus 'in the spirit' and therefore gives him not just an earthly title, but also a heavenly title.

Up to this point in time, Jesus had delivered his doctrine to his disciples in a manner easily understood through the five senses of the physical world, in veiled language:

"These things have I spoken unto you in proverbs: but the time cometh, when I shall no more speak unto you in proverbs, but I shall show you plainly of the Father." (**St John 16:25**)

The people were taught in a simple way, using parables:

"All these things spake Jesus unto the multitude in parables; and without a parable spake he not unto them." (**St Matthew 13:34**)

Mark summarises this in his account:

"And when he was alone, they that were about him with the twelve asked of him the parable. And he said unto them, Unto you it is given to know the mystery of the kingdom of God: but unto them that are without, all these things are done in parables." (**St Mark 4:10-12**)

Here, Jesus is explaining to the disciples that the time is fast approaching when he will be able to speak to them about heavenly matters, which are invisible; about matters which will by far surpass all things on this earth which are subject to corruption. He will soon be able to disclose details of God's world of angels within the rainbow mansions. He promises to be seen as never before, untouched by human hands and to be heard as never before; he promises to reveal a place where nothing grows old, looking forward to the time when he will drink spiritual wine with them:

"But I say unto you, I will not drink henceforth of this fruit of the vine, until that day when I drink it new with you in my Father's kingdom." (**St Matthew 26:29**)

The disciples longed for the truth and knowledge, never fully understanding that this could only be unfolded after the death of Jesus. Jesus could only pass on this knowledge after his Resurrection and Ascension, as a fully-materialised spirit. Only then would the disciples break through the barrier of the material world.

This is why Jesus gave John, James and Peter this order, at the Transfiguration:

"And as they came down from the mountain, Jesus charged them, saying, Tell the vision to no man, until the Son of man be risen again from the dead." (**St Matthew 17:9**)

These three disciples witness Jesus as a fully-materialised

spirit, when he is 'out of the body', at the Transfiguration. The next time that they see Jesus as a full materialisation is together with the other disciples in the upper room. Only then are the disciples able to begin to grasp the true meaning of the plain words of Jesus as he is eventually able to grant to them the secret of the Kingdom of God.

"To whom also he shewed himself alive after his passion by many infallible proofs, being seen of them forty days, and speaking of the things pertaining to the kingdom of God." **(Acts 1:3)**

The gospel of Bartholomew tells us:

"At that time before the Lord Jesus Christ suffered, all the disciples were gathered together, questioning him and saying: Lord show us the mystery in the heavens. But Jesus answered and said unto them: If I put not off the body of flesh I cannot tell you. But after that he had suffered and risen again, all the apostles looking upon him, durst not question him, because his countenance was not as it had been aforetime, but showed forth the fullness of power."

Jesus made no less than eleven appearances during the forty days following his Resurrection and Ascension. Proof of the words of Jesus has been recorded in the gospels of some of the less well-known disciples, discovered at the Nag Hamâddi caves. These alternative gospels from for example, Thomas, Bartholomew, James and Philip, are more direct, liberal and spiritually advanced than the four synoptic gospels of the Bible. Many of the subjects I have covered in this book are to be found in these accounts; I was very moved to read some of these gospels. With my insight into spiritual matters I found them to be (what I have so far managed to read) not complicated or confusing but easy to understand. These alternative gospels contain many of the themes featured in the synoptic gospels, including the major theme, i.e. that Jesus came to teach us all about the afterlife, yet the style of writing is, for me, so very different. I feel more freedom and truth in these writings; the language is more flowery. These alternative gospels have been translated in a more spiritual language; the messages are clear and positive. I now feel, having made the comparison, that the four major gospels must have been edited or censored, thus holding people to the rules of a religion, rather than to the truth.

The last recorded appearance of Jesus 'in the spirit', according to John, is on the shore of Tiberias. It is significant in that it is here that Jesus hands over authority to Peter to lead the disciples to become 'fishers of men'. John does not recognise the Ascension after this event, in fact he makes no reference to the Ascension after forty days; he knows that Jesus rose on the third day.

John tells us:

"And many other signs truly did Jesus in the presence of his disciples, which are not written in this book. But these are written, that ye might believe that Jesus is the Christ, the Son of God; and that, believing ye might have life through his name." **(St John 20:30-31)**

"And there are also many other things which Jesus did, the which, if they should be written every one, I suppose that even the world itself could not contain the books that should be written. Amen." **(St John 21:25)**

I conclude this chapter with words from the famous historian, Josephus, who lived at the time of Jesus:

"About that time lived Jesus, a wise man, if man he may be called, for he did wonderful works - a teacher of those who joyfully received the truth. He won to himself many Jews and many Greeks. He was the Christ, and though Pilatus condemned Him to death He was our Messiah and appeared on the third day."

Chapter 6
"CHANGING ROOMS"

There is a humorous side to death and the spiritual side of life. I would now like to share with you, in a light-hearted way, some of my own life experiences:

During the autumn of 1969 my father was taken ill with thrombosis and heart disease and he was taken to Selly Oak Hospital in Birmingham. His condition deteriorated after three or four days and so my brother and I took turns to sit with him through the night. After spending several nights at the hospital, I realised that there was a 'pecking order' for the beds on the ward - a game of musical beds! When a patient was deemed to be about to die, his bed would be moved to the end of the ward, next to the office used by the nursing staff. The doctors were 'spot-on' each time; a patient would be moved to the end bed and sure enough would pass away within the next 24 hours.

I approached the ward with dread each time, in case I found Father in that end bed for his last hours. Although I knew that he was very ill, I remained confident as his aura did not reveal to me that he was about to pass away into the heavenly mansions. This was an all-male ward of mostly heart cases and each time a patient died my father would be moved along, according to his condition. He would get to know some of the other patients around him and when they disappeared he would ask me where they had gone. Knowing by now that this was the ward where these men were to spend the last days of their lives, I simply told him that they had gone home. After three weeks the dreaded end bed was given to my dad; he was by now slipping in and out of a semiconscious state and had, according to the doctor, 'taken a turn for the worse'. However, my experience of reading auras told me that his time had not yet come. That night, it was my turn to sit with my father and I noticed a new gentleman in the bed opposite. At about two o'clock in the morning, the curtains drawn around his bed and above all the moans and groans of men trying to breathe with the aid of oxygen masks, I overheard his conversation. He spoke in such an informal and relaxed manner that I assumed that he was talking to someone very close to him. I soon realised, however, that I was listening to just one side of the conversation - his was the only voice I could hear. He spoke with a mellow Irish accent and as he spoke his voice became clearer and clearer. I heard his final words: "Wait for me, Annie; I am coming with you - help me up!". I felt so uncomfortable and I was just about to go across to him, when I heard an almighty crash. He had knocked over his locker and pulled down the curtain rail from around the bed. The man was lying, dead, on the floor. Early next morning his son and daughter came and I gathered that they were Catholics. The duty nurse brought me a cup of tea and when she had returned to her office, the daughter asked me if she could have a word. She asked if I had been there all night and if I had been there when her father had been found dead. I realised that the nurses had been kind enough to not add to their grief by mentioning that he had fallen from his bed. The daughter was very upset about her father and asked me if he had been in any distress at the end. I told her that he had not been alone as he passed and about his conversation with Annie. The tears rolled down her face as she explained that her mother, who had passed away a few years before, was called Annie.

The following night I decided to give my brother a rest and to sit with my dad again. Late into the evening the doctor came to the ward on his rounds. He was a tall, elderly gentleman with white hair and very thick eyebrows. He poked his head through the gap in the curtains and looked at me; he raised his eyebrows (and they looked to me like two large caterpillars ready to race across his forehead), "He will go comfortably," he said, and with that he wrote something on the clipboard at the end of the bed. This was one of the few times that I actually strained, in desperation, to see the details of an aura. I could not see what the doctor could see and I tried to force my gift to discover more. For the first time in years I questioned what I was seeing; I doubted my judgement and suddenly lost faith in my ability to accurately read auras. I knew from the reaction of the doctor that he thought that Father was not going to live through the night. As I settled down for the night in the large comfortable armchair next to the bed, I studied my father. Even though his aura showed that he was a very sick man, it was definitely a little brighter. I wondered if this was just wishful thinking or was my interpretation affected by the emotion of my love for my father?

Dad had not been one to eat much fruit and he rarely ate oranges. During that night as he began to stir, he asked the time and also asked if he could have an orange. As I was peeling an orange for him, my head filled with questions: Was he allowed to eat an orange and would he choke? Should I call a nurse or fetch a bedpan? As my father had always been a drinking man, I would have been a lot less shocked if he had asked for a pint of beer! I would have been quite prepared to wake the local pub landlord in order to grant that request - not because I believed that this would have been the last request of a dying man, but because I now knew that the doctor had been wrong. From then on Father was bombarded, while in hospital, with an endless supply of oranges!

The doctor, who had earlier raised his eyebrows in sympathy, returned on his rounds the following evening to see that Dad was still playing musical beds and had been moved back to the middle of the ward. I volunteered, out of curiosity, to stay with Dad for a third night, hoping that the same doctor would be on duty. Sure enough he was and he came straight over to Dad and said, "Well, I didn't expect to see you here this evening." My father, not realising what the doctor meant by this, replied, "I couldn't go home today; the wife hasn't got the bed downstairs for me to sleep in, yet"

My father was allowed to come home from the hospital in February 1970; I knew that this was to allow him to die in the comfort of his own home. After a couple of weeks, his aura finally started to fade. Although my mother realised that he would not be with us for much longer, she hoped that he would live to the end of the summer. One Tuesday evening I could see that he had just a few hours left. So I took it upon myself to inform other family members - so that they could come and say goodbye, if they wished. My father passed away peacefully in the early hours of the next morning.

Years ago, I had some close neighbours who supplied me with milk from their dairy cows for my dogs. This family consisted of the parents, their two sons in their twenties, and the grandfather - an intelligent old gentleman still very much in good health. The two young men used to come and spend time at my place, while I tended to the greyhounds and we would chat and exchange stories. I was

82

able to read their auras and successfully predict things about them and their friends. They did not realise or understand my spiritual gift. I can recall several occasions when they came back to me with the news that something that I had predicted had in fact happened. They wanted to know how I knew these things and how I could do that! The eldest boy would often tell me of his strange aunt, who claimed to be a witch and to be able to predict the future. He was ready to have a confrontation with her and asked if I would call on them when she next came to visit. It had always been an ambition of mine to meet a real live witch, and so I agreed.

One day the boys called for me to go back to their house with them as Auntie Witch had arrived - not on a broomstick but in a very large, smart Dormobile (apparently bought from the proceeds of her fortune-telling business!). I realised that not only did the boys want a second opinion on their aunt but also wanted to ridicule her a little, if they could. They had in their innocence, gained some respect for me; they looked forward to our meeting with great excitement. Apparently, Auntie had already been told about the neighbour, a greyhound trainer, who had become a family friend. As I walked into the yard, she opened the kitchen window and shouted, "Hello, you must be John!". Not being by nature a very serious person, I replied, "Wow! That's good! How do you do that?" Immediately we, that is, the two boys and I, fell about laughing and could not go into the house - we found it hysterical!

A few months later, Auntie came to visit again. I went to the house to collect the milk and was invited in for a cup of tea; it was about ten o'clock in the morning. I was drawn to look at Grandad. Auntie Witch was his daughter and was there to make arrangements to take him away for a few days, some time during the following week. However, witch or no witch, she failed to see what I could see in her own father - his aura was fading and was starting to crack on one side. The two boys helped me to carry the buckets of milk to my place, which was only a five minute walk away. When we reached my home I told them what I had seen, but made them promise not to say anything. Just after one o'clock, the eldest boy, white as a sheet, came running back into my yard and said that Grandad had just died in the armchair.

Meeting new people has always made me feel very uncomfortable and this reminds me of the time when I was invited to a friend's house for tea. I noticed on the sideboard a photograph of a small dog. From where I was sitting, it was difficult to identify the breed. My friend's mother had made some tea and placed the tray, containing the cups and teapot, etc., on a small table between my friend's father and me. As we were chatting, I noticed a small Jack Russell type terrier at the side of the settee, trying to attract my attention. I could see that my chair was different from the three piece suite though I was very comfortable, sitting almost into the bay window. As the lady of the house handed me a cup of tea, I noticed the brown and white terrier again. Being a greyhound trainer, I did not make a fuss of pet dogs; they seemed somewhat trivial and out of place to me. Even today I find that I fail to respond to pet dogs when I meet them. I have now been retired from greyhound training for many years, but I still have a great passion for animals. I was very skilled in my work and my greyhounds always had great respect for me. Discipline was the key to their routine of exercise, feeding, grooming, massage and toileting. In that respect this small terrier held no fascination for me. I did wonder however, how it kept appearing so quickly and then disappearing from view. I held my cup and saucer and as I was about to lift the cup from the saucer, I saw the dog again, looking straight into my eyes. More out of politeness than wanting to fuss the dog, I thought that I ought to acknowledge that I had noticed him. With that, he scurried towards me and leapt into my lap! I was so startled that I jumped up, spilling tea all over myself. My friend, his mother and father all stared at me in stunned silent amazement. I was so embarrassed and I remember saying, "You won't believe this, but a Jack Russell terrier just jumped into my lap!" As all this was happening, I knew that this was a spirit dog. Even so, I was far too slow in my reactions and was now covered in tea! The woman asked me to describe the dog, which I could do in great detail; I explained that its tail had been docked and yet still seemed too long for a Jack Russell. The family smiled at one another. It emerged that this dog had been put to sleep a few weeks earlier and I had been sitting on his chair - apparently he would sit on the headrest of this chair and look out of the window. This dog had been given to the family because of its odd appearance - it had only a three-quarter tail.

One Sunday evening I arranged to go to a special service at a local church. I did all the usual things in preparation: ate dinner early, had a bath and changed clothes, etc. With an hour to spare, I sat back in the armchair and fell fast asleep. When I woke up, it was too late to go to the service. The next day I was in the village - where the service had taken place, with my wife. We spoke to two people who claimed (independently) that they had seen me in church the night before. I tried in vain to convince them both that I had not left home, because I fell asleep but the more I protested, the more details I was given.

This is just one example of something that has happened to me many times over the years. I have often been told that I was seen at a particular function or place, when in fact I was at home, or somewhere else. More often than not, I have been spotted somewhere I planned to go, but did not, for whatever reason. I only have the other person's word for this as I have no recollection of any of these other outings. I must stress, however, that those who report back would have been companions at these events and therein lies the link. I can offer no other explanation.

As a child, I had great difficulty explaining to my mother about (what I now know to be) my gifts of the spirit. I was naturally very excited by the realisation that not everyone shared these experiences. As the significance of the colours of the aura became clearer to me, I began to notice the colours of nature.

As a boy, I would spend hours watching my pigeons displaying their coloured feathers; the cock birds would fill their throats with air and puff out their chests, to produce that wonderful trill! I have always been amazed to see those spiritual colours of the rainbow in the feathers around their necks. This brings to mind the story of Noah and the dove: It was the dove that brought an olive branch back to Noah, as a sign that the flood had subsided. This dove would have been the first to witness the rainbow and the birds of the dove family reflect the colours of the rainbow in their plumage.

I was similarly fascinated by the colours produced by oil or petrol in water. When it rained I would purposely walk out into the road; I lived on a large council estate, where it seemed everyone was an amateur mechanic. The road was covered with patches of oil and petrol and when the rain ran through these spillages the emergent colours intrigued me.

Looking at a rainbow in the sky reminded me of the colours I could see around the heads of the people around me, in their auras. I was, therefore, naturally drawn to these colours and this became an important part of my life. As I was not able to talk about this with my mother, I decided to share this in a different way.

After leaving school, I earned a good wage so decided that it was time my mother had a colour television and got rid of her old black and white Ferguson set. I found a shop offering a colour television for a trial period and ordered one. I asked for it to be delivered on Saturday morning, when I would be at home. I had to explain that my mother could be a little tricky about change. The man in the shop assured me that she would be delighted with her new colour set. Saturday morning arrived and I told my mother what I had arranged; she was very restless until there was a knock at the door and at that point she took control in her usual fashion. She answered the door and, announcing who she was, invited the man with his television into the sitting room. Mother sat in her chair and watched intently as the man carefully set up the beautiful new colour television with a 21" screen and teak surround. Every Saturday Mother liked a flutter on the horses and so she requested the racing channel (BBC). For the first time in her life, Mother was looking at horses in three or four different shades of chestnut and all the vibrant colours of the jockeys' silks. After just a couple of minutes however, Mother was holding her head in her hands. The TV man looked at me and I looked at him. Mother cried, "I can't look at all that colour - it's giving me a headache!" We tried in vain to calm her, but she insisted that the new set had to be disconnected and the old black and white set reinstated! Being a loving son, I had to respect her wishes and she settled down for the afternoon racing programme.

Mother had been so preoccupied in rearing four children through the war years before I came along, and she suffered all the hardships of life as a housewife without all the 'mod cons', that she had taken the colour in her life for granted. Looking out of the window or into her newspaper, she lived in the black and white world of the old Ferguson set. She was so shocked by the colour television she thought that all the colour of the world had somehow been put inside that set and that it was not real! She watched her black and white set for the rest of her life.

In September 1989, after twenty-five years in business, I flew out to the Far East with plans to settle in Thailand. I had suffered many traumatic life experiences and was feeling burdened and troubled by the stresses and strains of everyday life, it was all beginning to take its toll on me! My spiritual side had taken second place as the need to earn a living had taken priority. I was now filled with an overwhelming desire to 'find myself' and this became more important than the materialistic life I had been living.

After a few weeks of complete relaxation, good food and sunshine I began to see that my life was about to take a new turn. My girlfriend came to Thailand to live with me; after a few weeks in Pattaya, we decided to prepare for our wedding. The wedding dress and suit made, we hired a driver to take us on a tour of Thailand - a honeymoon before the wedding! This was to take a further three weeks, ending in Phuket, where we decided to get married.

I have already mentioned that as a boy in Birmingham, my best friend was my neighbour, Henry. I had last seen Henry when I was in my early twenties; he went into the RAF and I moved to Yorkshire. Here I was at the age of forty-four, living in Thailand, planning a wedding. The minister had agreed to organise the Christian ceremony, after the civil ceremony required under Thai law. The proprietor of the bungalows where we were staying, agreed to do the catering for the reception, the cake and to take photographs. The pressure was off, except for one last detail - what about a best man? We had no family or friends with us and it would not have felt right to break with tradition and ask a complete stranger!

Just days before the wedding, Lisa and I took a trip up into the hills. At one point we all climbed out of the minibus to take photographs of the spectacular sunset. Lisa left her handbag in the minibus for the few minutes that it took to take photographs. This was the one and only time, during the whole trip, that this bag had been left unattended. To be honest, I usually took charge of the bag and this had become something of a joke between us! We had heard the tales of the street crime and hill bandits of Thailand and so were very careful, using the hotel safe to hide our valuables, etc. Just the day before, we had been to the bank to exchange some traveller's cheques. When we arrived back at the bungalow, Lisa realised that our wallet had been emptied of all the money! There had been thousands of baht (Thai currency) in there - nearly £200 as I recall; the thief would have suddenly become very rich in Thai terms, as that sort of money could go a very long way at that time. We were quite hurt and saddened by this experience - you never think it's going to happen to you. We had regularly used this company for our excursions and by this time we were starting to get a feel for the place and to feel 'at home' in Thailand. It was obvious that the money had been taken by either the driver or the guide, the only other people on the trip were some ladies from Australia, who had left the bus as we did to take photographs. Lisa was so annoyed with herself for leaving the bag under the nose of an opportunist thief and she wanted to report the incident to the Thai police. My experience, however, was telling us not to bother; I knew that cases such as this often backfire on the innocent to protect the reputation of the locals. Apart from that, I was being pulled in a totally different direction and I knew that when that spiritual cord pulls it is better to go with the flow than to try to fight it.

So instead of going to the Police, we went out to dinner. We ate out somewhere different every evening and this evening was to be no exception in that respect. Lisa had become aware of my gifts by this time; we had known each other for almost a year and she was learning to recognise the signs and knew that something was about to happen. I explained that we had to go to a particular restaurant. It may have seemed ridiculous to anyone else, as there were so many restaurants; this was a tourist area catering for every conceivable taste. I knew that I was being 'pulled' to a certain restaurant, famous for its 'ribs' and so I dutifully answered the call. As we began tucking in to the most scrumptious spare ribs, I was excited at the prospect of this feast and momentarily forgot that eating was not the real order of the evening.

Sitting at a nearby table was another couple enjoying their meal. I was drawn to look at the woman; the man had his back to me. I had met this woman before - but where and when, who was she? Then it came to me. This was Margaret, the wife of my old pal, Henry, who I had last seen more than twenty years before. Henry then turned around; we both stood up and met in a clinch in the middle of the restaurant - two grown men, hugging and kissing, the tears flowing. I could hardly believe it - what a reunion - I had found my best man!

It turned out that Henry and Margaret were on a stopover in Phuket, so we spent the next few days together. If you had asked me to choose my best man, Henry would have been my man for the job - and here he was! We had travelled all around Thailand, we were now exploring the area around Phuket, never keeping to any particular agenda or plan - we could have been anywhere on that night!

My final story is a very special one and very dear to me heart. We decided to start a family and as Thailand, for many reasons which I will not go into here, is not the ideal place in which to rear children, we decided to return to England. Soon after our return, in the cottage where we are still living, Lisa became pregnant. Lisa is half Icelandic on her mother's side and retains a keen interest in her Icelandic roots and heritage. She named the child Freya, from Norse mythology. Just seven months later, Lisa was pregnant again and regularly monitored by the hospital, as Freya had been delivered prematurely, by Caesarean section. A scan revealed that this child was a boy.

One of my pastimes is listening to the music of the great tenors, past and present - my favourite of all being the Italian tenor, Beniamino Gigli. Another of my passions, as you will have realised by now, is studying the Bible. I named the boy therefore, while still in his mother's womb, Jacob Gigli. He was born, by a natural birth, on March 20th. Several months later, while listening to some of my music of Beniamino Gigli, I began to read of his life story from the record sleeve. Rarely have I felt the hairs on the back of my neck stand up as they did then and I felt all the colour drain from my face. I have seen some things in my time (I have told you of some of them): I have seen spirit people, witnessed many things on my travels, evaded death, suffered personal tragedy, etc., etc., but I was really taken aback by what I read. Such a discovery, I could not believe it - Jacob was born on the same day as my hero; Beniamino Gigli was born on March 20th!

There are many other stories I could have shared with you; I have given just a sample here. Each of these stories has a message and each reveals a different side of my spiritual personality. All have generated, for me, more questions than answers - questions of destiny, coincidence and spiritual gifts.

Many, especially those who are not aware of their spiritual side, would dismiss these events as coincidence or imagination. Yet if I were to put these experiences down to mere coincidence they would, by nature, disagree and claim that these experiences are not of the norm!

I consider that I am qualified to differentiate between coincidence and experiences controlled by gifts of the spirit - I leave it for you to decide!

Chapter 7
"THE CHAKRA SYSTEM"

Throughout the world there are many religions and cults that claim to acquire and develop gifts through meditation, physical and mental exercises and postures, breathing techniques, lights, music, scents and fasting, etc. Those who study psychic gifts work towards bringing to life certain vital centres within the psychic body. These psychic centres are known as Chakras. By definition, psychic means "outside the possibilities recognised by natural laws"; psychic gifts have come to mean those which cannot be explained by natural laws, i.e. not part of the normal functions of the physical body. I define psychic as spiritual and, as you are aware, spiritual gifts are natural and normal for me.

The Chakras cannot be seen by the naked eye, or by means of an X-ray; they are, therefore, not physical but spiritual. These students of psychic gifts aim to develop each Chakra with a view to improving a side of their personality or attaining higher spirituality. I would not claim that my gifts are psychic gifts - they are spiritual gifts.

We are told that these Chakras are dormant within the psychic body and can be opened by using one, or more, of the methods I have mentioned. The aim is to bring the spiritual on to a par with the physical, to lift the spiritual consciousness to the level of the physical consciousness - in an effort to balance and harmonise the physical and the spiritual. In most people, the spiritual is dominated by the physical.

Those who claim to possess psychic gifts are regarded, by society, as freakish. Some believe that at one time, many years ago, the Chakras were open for the majority rather than the few and that over time they have become dormant as we have become "civilised" - we have stopped living close to nature and we use the potential of our minds and bodies less and less. What then was the original purpose of these Chakras? If they were intended by God to be part of our lives, there would be no mystery. If these Chakras exist, dormant, within a person, is it part of the plan that they are brought to life? The big question for me, has been, "is it possible for psychic gifts to be "trained" to be active?" Throughout a man's life he is involved in sports, work and rest - how is it that these centres are not opened up naturally? Why is it that they, allegedly, open on request? I never asked for any of my spiritual gifts! I do not believe that any of this can be achieved by force. There must be a natural sensitivity in the first place and the more sensitive a person, the easier the task is to develop such gifts. If there were not gifts of the spirit in this world, it would not matter how hard a person tried to develop them - they could not be created! If these centres can be opened using the practices mentioned, this means that it is possible to "tap into" our spiritual side.

I have often wondered if one, or more, of these centres has been opened up in me. An obvious explanation for my gifts of the spirit comes from an accident I suffered as a small child, and that as a result of some malfunction, shock or disarrangement in my body, these gifts started to awaken in me. Before I was six months old, my older brother fell or jumped on me. I have no recollection of this incident. When I found a large scar across my abdomen as a boy I was naturally curious. When I asked my mother about this I was initially told that I had suffered a double rupture, but details were kept from me. Later, I was told more; as a baby I was left on the floor of the sitting room and my older brother was playing a game of jumping over baby brother. He fell or jumped on me, by accident. My stomach burst open until my bowels protruded. I suffered great blood loss and was rushed to hospital. I endured a long and potentially dangerous operation and I miraculously survived. This must have been a traumatic experience for one so young. It may be that I had a "near death" experience, that I was chosen not to die at that time, for some reason, and "returned" with added gifts. I believe that my spiritual gifts started to develop after this incident. However, I must stress here that I must have been spiritually sensitive by nature, in the first instance, for this to have happened. I would say that we all possess gifts of the spirit but only with a strong foundation of spiritual awareness (therein lies the advantage) is it possible to open up such gifts.

My main purpose, and the real interest for me, in looking at the Chakras, is to draw your attention to the colour system involved.

92

Each Chakra is represented by a colour of the rainbow and, just as with the order of the rainbow, moves from red, and as enlightenment is attained, to violet.

I have an understanding of the Chakra system through my knowledge of the spiritual side of martial arts, where certain exercises and techniques are employed to develop spiritual awareness. A similar system to the Chakra system is used by Tibetan monks who apply the same seven colours to seven specific areas of the body. The Chinese Chi system also links those same areas of the body to the same colours. The ancient Egyptian system, as shown in their *Book of the Dead*, describes a series of seven spiritual bodies in man.

It is a fact that God's colours are a common thread running through the religions of the world. The rainbow is the outward sign to mankind - for all to see - given to us by God. The colours of the rainbow, used in each of these systems, reveal the inner man. If we could all study these colours and their origins, from the knowledge that God has given us, we would gain the spiritual understanding that would bring us closer to God than any amount of prayer or meditation could.

The Chakra System is an ancient Indian tradition; the Chakras are seven in number and are situated along the spine, from the base of the spine to the top of the head and are linked directly to the colours in the aura and the rainbow wheel of the many mansions. I will now give a description of each of the Chakras, with my own interpretation of the colours, inspired by my understanding of God's colours:

Muladhara
This is known as the root Chakra at the base of the spine. Its colour is red and it is associated with physical activity and aggression.

Svadisthana
This Chakra is located just below the navel, but against the spine. Its colour is orange and it is associated with a sense of wanting and belonging.

Manipura
This Chakra is located behind the solar plexus (the network of nerves behind the stomach). Its colour is yellow and it is associated with the spirit body and emotions.

Anahata

This Chakra is in the spine, located behind the heart. Its colour is green, the colour of life and growth, and it is associated with wanting to stand out in a crowd.

Vishuddhi

This Chakra is behind the throat, in the spine, at the base of the neck. Its colour is blue and it is associated with uprightness and law.

Ajna

This Chakra is situated deep within the brain, behind the centre of the forehead and is known as the third eye. Its colour is indigo, a very deep spiritual blue, and it is associated with clairvoyance, giving of one's personality and sensitivity of the spirit.

Sahasrara

This Chakra is located at the top of the head and is said to be the seat of highest consciousness, depicted as a lotus with a thousand petals. Its colour is violet and it is associated with knowing the secret of life and being as one with the world.

This Chakra System holds many similarities, in my understanding, to the spiritual aura which surrounds our physical body, regarding colours indicating personality types. If these Chakras are indeed awakened, in the correct order, there may be a claim to spiritual gifts. There would definitely be some spiritual gain, which would be revealed in the aura.

Chapter 8
"A SIGHT TO SEE"

The greatest reader of the spiritual aura was Jesus Christ himself. Throughout the gospels there are many examples of this.

Jesus chose his disciples by reading their auras; we are not told of his reasons for choosing each one. These were simple men of nature with personalities untouched by thoughts of corruption. Some were fishermen: Simon (Peter), James, John and Andrew; Simon (Peter) and Andrew were brothers and James and John were brothers, sons of an affluent family. Nathanael (Bartholomew) was a learned man, Matthew allegedly a tax collector and Simon a Zealot. We are not given many specific details of these men in the Bible; some are not credited with any distinctive role and yet I feel that they must have had one. Others mentioned by name are Philip, James (son of Alphaeus) and Thaddaeus. Thomas became well known as "doubting" and Judas as the betrayer.

Jesus could see their qualities and potential in the colours of their auras. He was able to see at a glance the personalities he required; those who were going to learn to accept him were revealed to him. He had to be surrounded by those who would grow to love him and to absorb his teachings. Their past lives in terms of such things as occupations, tribes, etc. were of little interest to Jesus, these would be irrelevant to their future with him. His choices carried no prejudice of the day. There was no open invitation to everyone to become a disciple; Jesus invited those he wanted and not one declined his offer. Later, others would ask to become part of that immediate circle, but were refused. Therefore, as these disciples were to represent a cross-section of society, each and every person who gathered to hear Jesus would be able to identify with one or more of these men. These were the men who were to be instrumental in changing their world, by spreading the news of Jesus Christ, in word and deed. Jesus saw in these so-called ordinary men something extraordinary and gave them the chance to follow him and to learn the truth, at first hand. Jesus was able to look into their auras and see what ordinary human eyes could not see; he could see beyond the physical and into the spirit within. Being able to tap into their spirituality, he could single out those with the inherent capability to comprehend that he was the Messiah, the one sent to fulfil the scriptures. If this was happening today, even using the modern methods of in-depth interviews, psychological profiling, etc. that 'something special' that Jesus saw would never be detected. How he selected his disciples has always fascinated me and only he knew why. He chose twelve disciples, symbolic of the twelve tribes of Israel and in so doing, continued the theme of the scriptures, of God's chosen people. Even after the death of Judas, another was chosen to replace him to maintain a group of twelve.

The idea that Jesus gathered together just any group of people, in order to manipulate them and put some spell on them to turn them into perfect disciples, would be a complete contradiction of the whole of Christianity. The disciples were always regarded as ordinary men, working in his name. Jesus was able to aid the natural development of their spiritual gifts and so it became evident that his assessment of the twelve had been correct. He gave these men his authority to work on his behalf, not by supernatural powers, *"Go thou and preach the kingdom of God"* (**St Luke 10:60**)

Let us look at **St. John (1:38-51)** and see how Jesus began choosing his disciples:

"Then Jesus turned, and saw them following, and saith unto them, What seek ye? They said unto him, Rabbi, (which is to say, being interpreted, Master,) where dwellest thou? He saith unto them, Come and see. They came and saw where he dwelt, and abode with him that day: for it was about the tenth hour" (**St John 1:38-40**)

Here we have Jesus choosing the first two of his disciples: the first, Andrew and the other, who purposely withholds his name as he is the narrator, is John. Jesus asks them to 'come and see'; this is not just to see where he lives, but a much deeper invitation to witness the unfolding of a spiritual world. Jesus is able to read into their auras and they are chosen as the first ripples of what was to become a great ocean.

The third disciple to be chosen is Peter (Simon Peter). Andrew is so excited by the words of John the Baptist:

"I am the voice of one crying in the wilderness, Make straight the way of the Lord..." (**St John 1:23**)

96

"And looking upon Jesus as he walked, he saith, Behold the Lamb of God!" **(St John 1:36)**

Wanting to spread this remarkable news, the news that was in time to go global, Andrew goes to find his brother, Peter:

"One of the two which heard John speak, and followed him, was Andrew, Simon Peter's brother. He first findeth his own brother Simon, and saith unto him, We have found the Messias, which is, being interpreted, the Christ. And he brought him to Jesus. And when Jesus beheld him, he said, Thou art Simon the son of Jona: thou shalt be called Cephas, which is, by interpretation, A stone." **(St John 1:40-43)**

Jesus knows Peter, through his aura, without any introduction; he knows not only his name and family but can 'see' how he is going to develop, giving him the title 'Cephas', meaning stone. Later, Jesus says of him:

"And I say also unto thee. That thou art Peter, and upon this rock I will build my church ..." **(St Matthew 16:18)**

We now know that Jesus was accurate in his assessment of Peter; he was to become the strength of the twelve disciples and of all the disciples, most is written about Peter. I must stress that each time Jesus chose a disciple, using his gift, he knew much more about each of them than they knew about him. Jesus looked earnestly upon Peter with that royal gaze, and was able to read his innermost thoughts and see at a glance, in that simple fisherman, not only the weakness, but also the splendid greatness of the man.

Preparing for his return to Galilee, Jesus falls in with another young man, Philip:

"The day following Jesus would go forth into Galilee, and findeth Philip, and saith unto him, Follow me. Now Philip was of Bethsaida, the city of Andrew and Peter." **(St John 1:43-45)**.

Jesus has no need to ask any questions regarding Philip's background, etc. It is sufficient for him to read his aura and he invites Philip to follow him.

Philip, elated at finding the Messiah, is eager to share this news with his friend, Nathanael, and a fifth disciple is added to the band.

"Philip findeth Nathanael, and saith unto him, We have

97

found him of whom Moses in the law, and the prophets, did write, Jesus of Nazareth the son of Joseph. And Nathanael said unto him, Can there any good thing come out of Nazareth? Philip saith unto him, Come and see. Jesus saw Nathanael coming to him, and saith of him, Behold an Israelite indeed, in whom is no guile! Nathanael saith unto him, Whence knowest thou me? Jesus answered and said unto him, Before that Philip called thee, when thou wast under the fig tree, I saw thee. Nathanael answered and saith unto him, Rabbi, thou art the Son of God; thou art the King of Israel. Jesus answered and said unto him, Because I said unto thee, I saw thee under the fig tree, believest thou? Thou shalt see greater things than these. And he saith unto him, Verily, verily, I say unto you, Hereafter ye shall see heaven open, and the angels of God ascending and descending upon the Son of man." (St John 1:45-51)

Philip wants Nathanael to meet Jesus; we must assume that Philip knows Nathanael, but Nathanael does not know Jesus. Jesus, however, knows Nathanael instinctively and sums him up as one 'in whom is no guile'. Jesus explains that before Philip had introduced him, he had seen him under the fig tree. Able to read his nature in an instant he had already made up his mind about him before they met. There is no mystery here as we realise that when Jesus says "I saw thee", he is telling us that he saw his aura, and it is Jesus, not Philip, who then makes the choice of Nathanael as the next disciple. Nathanael is amazed and acknowledges Christ, recognising that this is no ordinary man. Jesus then promises Nathanael that he will witness much greater things in the future, in his company.

All through his ministry, as with these examples of some of his disciples, Jesus was able to identify people by name and discern their personality without introduction, by using his spiritual gift of reading the aura.

"And Jesus entered and passed through Jericho. And, behold, there was a man named Zaccheus, which was the chief among the publicans, and he was rich. And he sought to see Jesus who he was; and could not for the press, because he was of little stature. And he ran before, and climbed up into a sycamore tree to see him: for he was to pass that way. And when Jesus came to the

98

place, he looked up, and saw him, and said unto him, Zaccheus, make haste, and come down; for to-day I must abide at thy house. And he made haste, and came down, and received him joyfully. And when they saw it, they all murmured, saying, That he was gone to be guest with a man that is a sinner. And Zaccheus stood, and said unto the Lord; Behold, Lord, the half of my goods I give to the poor; and if I have taken any thing from any man by false accusation, I restore him fourfold. And Jesus said unto him, This day is salvation come to this house, forsomuch as he also is a son of Abraham. For the Son of man is come to seek and to save that which was lost." **(St Luke 19:1-11)**

Here again, Jesus knows all about Zaccheus without introduction and calls him by name. When a person meets a stranger for the first time, with that first glance or greeting, human nature will automatically react in certain ways. Personal information, such as a name, flows through physical thoughts and into the aura. In his eagerness Zaccheus sends out countless messages, which are picked up by Jesus as he looks up at him; all Jesus has to do is to look into his aura to know all about him. Jesus pays Zaccheus the highest compliment by publicly announcing that he too is a son of Abraham; Jesus has no regard for his position or reputation in society.

Please refer here to **St John 4:5** onwards for the account of the 'woman at the well'.

In the course of his travels, Jesus comes to the Samaritan town of Sychar, near to the land that Jacob gave to his son, Joseph. Feeling tired, Jesus sits by Jacob's well, his disciples having gone to the town to buy food. A Samaritan woman comes to the well to draw water and Jesus asks her for a drink. The woman answers:

"How is it that thou, being a Jew, askest drink of me, which am a woman of Samaria?" **(St John 4:9)**

Jews did not associate with Samaritans; Jesus however always disregards such social discrimination. The woman recognises that Jesus is a Jew by his dress and accent. Jesus, however, 'sees' so much more in her.

This woman, to be out alone at this time of day, may have been a woman of ill-repute. There were certain times of the day

99

when it was acceptable for women to go to the well. It was the custom for them to go in a group - there was safety in numbers. Perhaps she was avoiding the company of the other women or had been ostracised by them. It was usual to visit the well when it was cool; this meeting, between Jesus and the woman, took place at midday, when it would have been very hot. Jesus replies,

"If thou knewest the gift of God, and who it is that saith to thee, Give me to drink; thou wouldest have asked of him, and he would have given thee living water." (St John 4:10)

It would have been customary, in those times, for a stranger to request a drink from the local well. As we know, Jesus ignores local prejudice and makes a point of associating with those marginalised by society. Jesus opens up a conversation, which must have been a shock to this woman. What is unusual, is that the woman answers Jesus and enters into conversation with him, implying that she is not a decent, principled female. Jesus quickly lifts the mood on to a higher, more spiritual, level. He needs water to sustain his physical well-being. In return he is offering spiritual water and the knowledge of eternal life; if she had known of God's gift to us all and realised who it is asking for a drink, then she would have been the one to ask. John goes on:

"The woman saith unto him, Sir, thou hast nothing to draw with, and the well is deep: from whence then hast thou that living water? Art thou greater than our father Jacob, which gave us the well, and drank thereof himself, and his children, and his cattle?" (St John 4:11-13)

The woman is beginning to show an interest in what Jesus is saying and shows respect by addressing him as 'Sir'. She is not refusing him a drink; she seems, to me, to adopt a facetious attitude by almost saying, "who do you think you are?" She quotes Jacob, the great patriarch, father of the twelve tribes of Israel; the one who wrestled with God and had the famous dream of the ladder. This is Jacob's well; he had used it and even he had to use a bucket to draw water! She is confused and so Jesus goes on to explain:

"Jesus answered and said unto her, Whosoever drinketh of this water shall thirst again: But whosoever drinketh of the water that I shall give him shall never thirst; but the water that I shall give

him shall be in him a well of water springing up into everlasting life. The woman saith unto him, Sir, give me this water, that I thirst not, neither come hither to draw." **(St John 4:13-16)**

Jesus is warming to this woman and he knows that she is not lost. He, therefore, sets out to prove to her that he is someone far greater than her hero, Jacob. He calls her bluff and feeds her the line about her husband. She immediately reacts and brings to mind her relationships; the information is thrown up into her aura, which Jesus can see through the eye of faith. He is then able, without reproach or condemnation, to give details of her life:

"Jesus saith unto her, Go, call thy husband and come hither. The woman answered and said, I have no husband. Jesus said unto her, Thou hast well said, I have no husband: For thou hast had five husbands: in that saidst thou truly. The woman saith unto him, Sir, I perceive that thou art a prophet." **(St John 4:16-20)**

The woman realises that Jesus has read her thoughts and she admits the truth and proclaims him a prophet. The woman contrives:

"Our fathers worshipped in this mountain; and ye say, that in Jerusalem is the place where men ought to worship." **(St John 4:20)**

The mountain, the woman speaks of, was called Gerizim and on this mountain the Samaritans built a rival to the Jerusalem Temple. It was destroyed by John Hycranus in 129 BC.

Jesus sees that she is one who will rush out and repeat his words and spread the news. He therefore takes this opportunity to preach to her of eternal life:

"Jesus saith unto her, Woman, believe me, the hour cometh, when ye shall neither in this mountain, nor yet at Jerusalem, worship the Father. Ye worship ye know not what: we know what we worship: for salvation is of the Jews. But the hour cometh, and now is, when the true worshippers shall worship the Father in spirit and in truth: for the Father seeketh such to worship him. God is a Spirit: and they that worship him must worship him in spirit and in truth." **(St John 4:21-25)**

Jesus now goes on to declare, for the first time, (and to a woman!), that he is the Messiah:

"The woman saith unto him, I know that Messias cometh,

which is called Christ: when he is come, he will tell us all things. Jesus saith unto her, I that speak unto thee am he." (**St John 4: 25-27**)

One of the most important events in the ministry of Jesus is the healing of the woman with the issue of blood:

"...But as he went the people thronged him. And a woman having an issue of blood twelve years, which had spent all her living upon physicians, neither could be healed of any, came behind him, and touched the border of his garment: and immediately her issue of blood stanched. And Jesus said, who touched me? When all denied, Peter and they that were with him said, Master, the multitude throng thee and press thee, and sayest thou, Who touched me? And Jesus said, Somebody hath touched me: for I perceive that virtue is gone out of me. And when the woman saw that she was not hid, she came trembling, and falling down before him, she declared unto him before all the people for what cause she had touched him, and how she was healed immediately. And he said unto her, Daughter, be of good comfort; thy faith hath made thee whole; go in peace." (**St Luke 8: 42-49**)

In the crowd following Jesus there is a woman who has been bleeding for twelve years. She has spent all her money on physicians, hoping to find a cure, without success - which may well have added to her problems. This has been a common problem for women throughout history; women suffer in silence and hide their discomfort. This woman, having endured pain and indignity for such a long time, is by now at her wits' end. Her faith has guided her to seek out the greatest physician of them all - Jesus Christ. Many cases, hideously deformed by disease, including the lepers, would come before the divine healer; the disabled would look him in the face and the handicapped would grasp his hand. According to Luke, who was himself a physician, this woman is unable to do this. In her situation, according to the laws and customs of the time, she is unfit to share any normal relationships; she is "ceremonially unclean". For her to disclose the nature of her complaint, in public and to a predominantly male crowd, would have been acutely embarrassing and even more humiliating than her actual affliction. Nevertheless, she is moved in

102

desperation to reach for that divine cure.

The crowd is large and moving at speed towards another plea for help; the daughter of Jairus is dying. This woman has such amazing inner strength to struggle in this crowd, which contains the Pharisees (in their splendid robes of office, always ready to pounce like hyenas on innocent prey). They follow and listen, watch and wait to pick at, and change, the very meaning of the royal words of Jesus. The disciples are also close to their master, never realising that he is always safe.

The woman takes her chance, hoping for an unknown blessing; she lunges and touches the hem of his cloak. Instantly she gains her desire and is healed. She shrinks back into the crowd, unnoticed by any of those following Jesus, including the disciples - unnoticed by all, except Jesus. He perceives that some healing power has drained from him, feels the magnetic force of one humble spirit drawing power from another. This is the divine spirit reaching automatically, without consent, without the use of the eye or the touch of the physical body; healing power so divine that it can respond to the most timid of faith, flowing from the very spirit that belongs to God. The woman is able to draw from this power, without words or command from Jesus - a power so easy to tap into which requires only genuine faith.

Jesus asks who has touched him. His words sound absurd to the disciples as everyone is pushing and jostling for a better view of him. Jesus knows the difference between the crowding of curiosity and a simple touch of genuine faith. Jesus scans the many faces of the crowd and his eyes are drawn to the woman. He can see her aura, glowing; he can "see" who touched him. He can see that power has been transferred, from him into her. He has given freely of himself and the woman, because of her faith, has drawn from him. It is spiritual, not physical, that which she has taken and it is therefore revealed in her aura. She now shines, having been dull for so many years, as her true personality returns.

The woman now knows that she is not hidden amongst the crowd and that Jesus recognises her. She is overwhelmed by his majestic stare, comes to him and flings herself at his feet. He gives her the courage to admit to her actions and to disclose the nature of her condition, now miraculously healed.

In defiance of the law and despite being 'unclean', feeling weak and unwell, she has touched Jesus. The punishment for such an act would normally have been stoning . Jesus is so spiritually evolved that to touch his clothing is enough to draw sufficient power to heal this woman. A mere touch has cleansed her, but her touch has not polluted Jesus in any way.

The incident involving the adulterous woman again illustrates the power of his spiritual gifts and shows us how Jesus is instantly able to gauge a situation and its outcome.

"And the scribes and Pharisees brought unto him a woman taken in adultery; and when they had set her in the midst, They say unto him, Master, this woman was taken in adultery, in the very act. Now Moses in the law commanded us, that such should be stoned: but what sayest thou? This they said, tempting him, that they might have to accuse him. But Jesus stooped down, and with his finger wrote on the ground, as though he heard them not. So when they continued asking him, he lifted up himself, and said unto them, He that is without sin among you, let him first cast a stone at her. And again he stooped down, and wrote on the ground. And they which heard it, being convicted by their own conscience, went out one by one, beginning at the eldest, even unto the last: and Jesus was left alone, and the woman standing in the midst. When Jesus had lifted up himself, and saw none but the woman, he said unto her, Woman, where are those thine accusers: hath no man condemned thee? She said, No man, Lord. And Jesus said unto her, Neither do I condemn thee: go, and sin no more." **(St John 8:3-12)**

Here we have a mob of fanatics, bent on trapping Jesus; they want him arrested and handed over to the authorities. The Scribes and the Pharisees bring a woman to Jesus, as he is teaching in the temple. This woman is the bait, supposedly caught by chance in the act of adultery; for me, it all points to a 'set-up.'

Jesus 'sees' all that he needs to know as the mob is approaching, he knows what is coming. He can read the rage in their auras; many bands of red with blue, or red with green, the colour of murky seaweed, darting in and out. He can see the plan and that they are all of the same mind; he is the one that they want to accuse, not the woman.

They all fail to see his simple gesture as he runs his finger through the dust. He knows that by the time he has given his answer his message will have blown away; such a mark is quickly covered over and forgotten. Jesus is, as usual, one step ahead and can see that for all the rantings and ravings this will all blow over very quickly. The mob believes that it has a concrete case and that whatever the outcome they have trapped Jesus. If he disregards the sacred law and lets the woman go, he will himself be accused of heresy or treason; for contradicting the law he will be sent before the Sanhedrin and then the Procurator. If, on the other hand, he is ruthless and condemns the woman to be stoned, he risks losing those followers touched by his tenderness.

Having anticipated all this, Jesus responds. His answer is profound:

"He that is without sin among you, let him first cast a stone at her." (**St John 8:7**)

This line has stood the test of time. Jesus makes his point again and scribbles in the dust - by the time he looks up, the crowd has dispersed. Only the woman remains. Her accusers, who could have taken the law into their own hands and stoned her, now accuse themselves.

There are several accounts of Jesus using his aura to repel his enemies; he could recognise an enemy by its aura. He could do this because he was perfectly human, a physical man with gifts of the spirit, not because he was supernatural. His aura was so spiritually evolved that he could extend it, as he brought to mind all that was righteous, by proclaiming with authority who he was. The best example of this was at his arrest in the garden of Gethsemane:

"Jesus therefore, knowing all things that should come upon him, went forth, and said unto them, Whom seek ye? They answered him, Jesus of Nazareth. Jesus saith unto them, I am he. And Judas also, which betrayed him, stood with them. As soon then as he had said unto them, I am he, they went backward, and fell to the ground." (**St John 18:4 -7**)

Jesus knows everything that is to happen to him, not because of his knowledge of the prophecies of the scriptures, but from his sensitive gifts. The simple words "I AM" expand his aura and instantly swell his spirit with spiritual power. His whole being ignited, he is filled and draws on this power. Nothing is more powerful than these few, profound words; these words are the most authoritative in the Bible. His gentle answer has a strength greater than the cutting east wind; God is in that tranquil voice. Jesus is untouchable; these words put his unseen defence mechanism into operation. They produce, with a sudden start, such terror that his enemies are repelled and struck to the ground.

I must explain the significance and importance of the words I AM, which run like a velvet thread through the Bible.

"And Moses said unto God, Who am I, that I should go unto Pharaoh, and that I should bring forth the children of Israel out of Egypt? And he said, Certainly I will be with thee; and this shall be a token unto thee, that I have sent thee: When thou hast brought forth the people out of Egypt, ye shall serve God upon this mountain. And Moses said unto God, Behold, when I come unto the children of Israel, and shall say unto them, The God of your fathers hath sent me unto you; and they shall say to me. What is his name: what shall I say unto them? And God said unto Moses, I AM THAT I AM: and he said, Thus shalt thou say unto the children of Israel, I AM hath sent me unto you." **(Exodus 3:11 -15)**

This is part of the account of the Exodus, when God first reveals his divine name to Moses. The words "I AM" represent the authority of God and carry all that is divine and righteous. No other words have this power and authority upon this earth. With God there was no beginning and there will be no end. He was, is, and will always be. These words confirm the eternal existence of God.

Jesus uses the authority given to him by God, throughout the gospels, by using the words "I AM", for example:

"I AM the light of the world

I AM the door of the sheep

I AM the good shepherd

106

I AM the resurrection and the life

I AM the way, the truth, the life

I AM the true vine

I AM the bread of life

I AM from above

I AM not of this world"

In Jesus and Abraham, Jesus again uses the power of "I AM" to escape his enemies:

"Then said the Jews unto him, Now we know that thou hast a devil. Abraham is dead, and the prophets; and thou sayest, If a man keep my saying, he shall never taste of death. Art thou greater than our father Abraham, which is dead? And the prophets are dead: whom makest thou thyself? Jesus answered, If I honour myself, my honour is nothing: it is my Father that honoureth me; of whom ye say, that he is your God: Yet ye have not known him; but I know him: and if I should say, I know him not, I shall be a liar like unto you: but I know him, and keep his saying. Your father Abraham rejoiced to see my day: and he saw it, and was glad. Then said the Jews unto him, Thou art not yet fifty years old, and hast thou seen Abraham? Jesus said unto them, Verily, verily, I say unto you, Before Abraham was, I am. Then took they up stones to cast at him: but Jesus hid himself, and went out of the temple, going through the midst of them, and so passed by." **(St John 8:52 -end)**

Again, Jesus finds himself in a situation where the Jews are threatening to stone him. He is preaching to them of the many mansions. To prove his point he tells them of Abraham and the prophets, who now exist in the spirit world. He explains that he came to Earth from that place. Abraham lives on there, and is joyfully witnessing the life of Jesus. The assembled crowd cannot accept what Jesus is saying. These people think only in earthly terms,

107

whereas Jesus is speaking of the spiritual. Sensing their hostility and intention, he tells them, "before Abraham was, I am", to explain his point.

By using "I AM", these divine words of authority, he draws on the power of God and this enables him to safely leave the temple. He cannot just vanish! The power created by these words expands his aura and alters his facial expression; the crowd is overwhelmed and momentarily stunned. Jesus is given the opportunity to repel these enemies as he forges a pathway through the "midst" of them and is able to escape another stoning.

Jesus goes to teach in the temple during the Feast of Tabernacles, also known as the Feast of Shelters, which is held to commemorate the passage of the Israelites through the wilderness.

"Now about the midst of the feast Jesus went up into the temple, and taught. And the Jews marvelled, saying, How knoweth this man letters, having never learned? Jesus answered them, and said, My doctrine is not mine, but his that sent me." (**St John 7:14-17**)

"Then cried Jesus in the temple as he taught, saying. Ye both know me, and ye know whence I am: and I am not come of myself, but he that sent me is true, whom ye know not. But I know him: for I am from him, and he hath sent me. Then they sought to take him: but no man laid hands on him, because his hour was not yet come." (**St John 7:28 -31**)

The Jews in the temple know all about his background and so are amazed at his teachings. To listen to him is to disarm, and therefore weaken, the very aim of their mission to kill him. The power of his aura unnerves their strength and paralyses their will. Jesus preaches of his divine origins and tells the people that he has not come of his own accord but has been sent by God and that these words come from God. By quoting "I AM", Jesus expands his aura and is shielded; he is therefore able to repel his enemies.

Many times, through the gospel of St John, we read, as here, that his hour was not yet come - especially when Jesus succeeds in avoiding danger. Jesus knows that now is not the time for him to die. He has not yet fulfilled his purpose, as prophesied in the scriptures.

There is so much more to be done, so much more that has to happen; his work is not yet complete in preparing the disciples and he knows this. No man laid hands on him , simply because they are not meant to! Always aware of the outcome, Jesus helps himself and calls on the protection produced by the power of his aura and is able to call a halt to the proceedings.

Jesus has been sent to fulfil God's plan, through which he is to achieve certain objectives. Man has no power and is helpless in changing what is predestined. This incident proves that God is always in control and that no harm can come to Jesus; no-one can take his life until he gives it. God is in charge and so nothing is to divert Jesus from his course; nothing will happen to Jesus until God allows it to happen. To emphasise the fact that the life and ministry of Jesus is controlled, we look to the final act - to the Last Supper - which leads to the arrest, trial and the Crucifixion of Jesus Christ.

"Now before the feast of the passover, when Jesus knew that his hour was come that he should depart out of this world unto the Father ..." (St John 13:1)

"And he came to Nazareth, where he had been brought up: and, as his custom was, he went into the synagogue on the sabbath day, and stood up for to read. And there was delivered unto him the book of the prophet Esaias. [=Isaiah] And when he had opened the book, he found the place where it was written. The Spirit of the Lord is upon me to preach the gospel to the poor; he hath sent me to heal the broken-hearted, to preach deliverance to the captives, and recovering of sight to the blind, to set at liberty them that are bruised. To preach the acceptable year of the Lord. And he closed the book, and he gave it again to the minister, and sat down. And the eyes of all them that were in the synagogue were fastened on him. And he began to say unto them, This day is this scripture fulfilled in your ears. And all bare him witness, and wondered at the gracious words which proceeded out of his mouth. And they said, Is not this Joseph's son? And he said unto them. Ye will surely say unto me this proverb, Physician, heal thyself: whatsoever we have heard done in Capernaum, do also here in thy country. And he said, Verily I say unto you, No prophet is accepted in his own country. But I tell you of a truth, many widows were in Israel in the days of Elias, when the

109

heaven was shut up three years and six months, when great famine was throughout all the land. But unto none of them was Elias sent, save unto Sarepta, a city of Sidon, unto a woman that was a widow. And many lepers were in Israel in the time of Eliseus the prophet; and none of them was cleansed, saving Naaman the Syrian. And all they in the synagogue, when they heard these things, were filled with wrath. And rose up, and thrust him out of the city, and led him unto the brow of the hill whereon their city was built, that they might cast him down headlong. But he passing through the midst of them went his way." **(St Luke 4:16-31)**

In the synagogue in Nazareth Jesus reads from the book of Isaiah **(Isaiah 61:1,2)** in which the coming of the Messiah is prophesied, seven hundred years before his birth. Jesus explains that he has been reading about himself - that he is the one who has come to fulfil the scriptures. The people know his earthly roots, but know nothing of his divine connections or spiritual gifts. By discussing his family they try to ridicule and discredit him. Having an innate understanding of human nature, he expects them to demand proof of his claim by asking him to perform one of the miracles that they have only heard about ; he gives us the now famous line:

"No prophet is accepted in his own country." **(St Luke 4:24)**

We all know from personal experience that people will travel outside their own area to buy, for example, a particular vehicle or pedigree dog, when the same could be bought locally. Man has a natural distrust or jealousy of his neighbour. So, as here with Jesus, a prophet is not honoured or recognised in his home town.

Jesus is known by these people as a humble village carpenter, which is considered one of the least valued occupations of the time. They are also aware that he has not been taught in the schools of the great rabbis. So where has all this expertise, knowledge and authority come from, suddenly? They wonder how the son of Joseph can claim to be the Messiah and naturally question this.

As Jesus quotes the scriptures, he compares himself to the great prophets - Elias (Elijah) and Eliseus (Elisha) - regarding the problem of familiarity . They travelled out of their own areas to heal, cure and perform miracles: Elijah and the woman of Sarepta and Elisha and Naaman, the Syrian. (These people still await the return of Elijah!) Jesus reminds them that these prophets helped not just their own race, but those in need. This offends and enrages the crowd. Claiming to be God's chosen people, they believe that these prophets were exclusive to the Jews, and it hurts to learn the truth.

The crowd rises against Jesus and forces him out of the town. They lead him to the brow of a hill, to throw him off, but he passes straight through them and walks away. Jesus does not resist the crowd, but permits the situation to go so far. He allows this mob to sink deeper and deeper into their own evil jealousy. Their perceived strength in their numbers and power in their raised voices, these people are completely unaware that they will soon be rendered helpless. Jesus identifies the murky colours of their auras back in the synagogue and knows he is to be rejected. It is these colours, the reds mingling with greens and blues, that are to prove their undoing. If they had heeded his words, the words of the seven hundred year old prophecy, and digested their meaning, they would have realised that this was to be a wasted journey.

Apart from his innocent gaze and chilling silence, there is always a noble, majestic authority about the presence of Jesus; full of grace he announces the first line of the prophecy:

"The Spirit of the Lord is upon me ..." (**St Luke 4:18**)

These words, of the prophecy of Isaiah, Jesus takes as his own to reveal that he is, in fact, the Messiah. They fill his spirit with power, automatically extending his aura, awarding him the protection he needs, and he can call on them at any time, to overcome his enemies. The angrier the people become, the weaker their auras become and this adds to the power of Jesus. As the crowd becomes weaker, he becomes stronger, and so there is no way that they are going to be able to inflict any harm on Jesus. Only he would have heard the angelic host descending from the heavens; only he would have felt the awesome surge of spiritual energy filling him from toe to head, as he delivers these words.

As they reach the brow of the hill, the raging mob is consumed with hatred and loathing; Jesus, whose aura is by now blazing like a cocoon of furnace heat, could easily have driven the mob over the side, like the swine at Gergesenes (see **St Matthew 8:28-33**). Jesus prefers to leave them with a mystery and, like a knife through butter, repels them with the power of his aura and escapes through the midst of them and goes on his way.

Jesus has good reason for allowing the mob to take him as far as the brow of the hill. If he had resisted, it may have caused a riot; his family and friends would have become victims of circumstance. They would obviously have rushed to support him and would have been harmed. Even at the point at which he is seemingly defenceless, Jesus retains control and is able to turn the tables. Again, they try to take him and again, he escapes right through their hands.

As I have explained, Jesus is able to do this by using the power of his aura and it is by this power that Jesus makes his escape as the maddened Jews in the temple pick up stones to stone him. It is this power that prevents the bold and bigoted officers of the Sanhedrin from arresting Jesus as he teaches in public during the Feast of the Tabernacles in Jerusalem. It is this power that causes his armed enemies to fall before him in the garden of Gethsemane.

To the disciples, as they were the privileged ones who witnessed his spiritual gifts, Jesus must have come across as a leader of extraordinary qualities. They must have seen far greater things than we have been told and St John tells us so:

"And many other signs truly did Jesus in the presence of his disciples, which are not written in this book." **(St John 20:36)**

I conclude this chapter, in which we have explored how Jesus could read others, with an account of Judas Iscariot, the disciple who from the outset:

"was destined to be lost, and this was to fulfil the scriptures." **(St John 17:12)**

"... Jesus knew from the beginning ... who should betray him ..." **(St John 6:24)**

"Have not I chosen you twelve, and one of you is a devil? He spake of Judas Iscariot the son of Simon: for he it was that should betray him, being one of the twelve." **(St John 6:70,71)**

Jesus was accurate in his assessment of the twelve, including Judas; he was with Jesus from the beginning and throughout his ministry. History tells us of underground movements against the

Romans, at this time, their aim to free the Israelites from the power of the Roman Empire. I believe Judas to be a member of such an organisation - chosen by Jesus, who knew all about him, to join the disciples. The Jews were awaiting a Messiah, to rid them of their oppressors, they were, however, expecting a great warrior and not a Messiah of mercy. Jesus, claiming to be the Messiah, building a reputation by speaking with such authority and performing miracles, was drawing the crowds. He was therefore, becoming a threat, not only to the priests and the Pharisees, but also to the Romans. From the point of view of the underground movement, it was then well worth attaching one of its members to Jesus.

For three years the disciples, including Judas, travelled on foot and slept rough; they were jostled in the everyday crowds and jeered at for being part of the band associated with a man the authorities were trying to trap. Judas may have been growing tired of words of forgiveness and kindness. It had come to the point where the authorities had regularly spied on Jesus and threatened him with arrest. Judas must have realised that eventually Jesus would be imprisoned or there would be a threat on his life. Tired of waiting, Judas decided to escalate the inevitable course of events, in the name of his cause.

Judas knew exactly who Jesus was, he knew that he was the Messiah, and not a warrior; he was well aware that Jesus could call on far greater powers. Having worked this out, Judas hatched a plan in a bid to overthrow the Romans. His aim was to force Jesus into a position where he would have to call on these powers. Judas believed that Jesus had the power to release the Jews and that he should do just that. It was never his intention to betray Jesus; yet Jesus had to be betrayed by one of his inner circle, not by a Roman, and so this became "the great betrayal". Judas, even though he was a disciple of Jesus and had received all his teachings, could not change what was to be. Jesus knew that he was to be betrayed and Judas, being someone with a credible motive, had been chosen for that purpose. Judas meant for Jesus to be placed in a situation where, in order to defend his God-given disciples, he would have to act and call for divine intervention. It was never his intention that Jesus be crucified, and as his plan backfired, he later committed suicide.

We are reminded of the extent of this power in the garden of

113

Gethsemane:

"Then said Jesus unto him, Put up again thy sword into his place: for all they that take the sword shall perish with the sword. Thinkest thou that I cannot now pray to my Father, and he shall presently give me more than twelve legions of angels? But how then shall the scriptures be fulfilled, that thus it must be?" (**St Matthew 26:52 -55**)

A legion meant, at this time, a unit in the Roman army of between three and six thousand men, and so this number multiplied by twelve would equal between thirty six and seventy two thousand angels! Jesus says that God would give him more than this; all he had to do was ask. We are told of the power of angels in the story of Lot and the two angels at Sodom:

"And they smote the men that were at the door of the house with blindness, both small and great: so that they wearied themselves to find the door. And the men said unto Lot, Hast thou here any besides? son in law, and thy sons, and thy daughters, and whatsoever thou hast in the city, bring them out of this place: For we will destroy this place, because the cry of them is waxen great before the face of the Lord; and the Lord hath sent us to destroy it." (**Genesis 19:11-14**)

Imagine then the potential power of more than seventy two thousand angels!

Judas thought that his actions would provoke some form of uprising or riot and that Jesus would have no option but to resist. Judas expected that at this point Jesus would call on such power! This was never going to happen, however. Jesus would not - could not - work against the word of God and he tells us so.

"But how then shall the scriptures be fulfilled, that thus it must be?" (**St Matthew 26:54**)

A genuine prophecy, handed down through the scriptures, being the word of God, cannot be altered. God gave his messages to his prophets (super-prophets as I like to call them) and we can read of these in the Bible. A true prophecy tells us of the future and as long as it has come from God (there have been and still are many false prophets, as you will know) then it will happen. If Jesus had called on the angels to come to his aid he would have been attempting

114

to break the chain of events mapped out for him and therefore he would have challenged the will of God.

Judas was put in charge of the common fund, the money the disciples needed for day-to-day expenses. Jesus gave this job to Judas, which allowed him the freedom of movement he required. Jesus was well aware of his activities within the underground movement and it is possible that Judas was passing money from the fund to this movement. Jesus, therefore, did not seek to restrict his movements.

"Then saith one of his disciples, Judas Iscariot, Simon's son, which should betray him, Why was not this ointment sold for three hundred pence, and given to the poor? This he said, not that he cared for the poor; but because he was a thief, and had the bag, and bare what was put therein." (**St John 12:4 -7**)

This quote illustrates the accepted image of Judas.

Judas was chosen by Jesus in the same way as the other disciples. By his aura Jesus knew his worth and it was therefore no coincidence that Judas was given charge of the common fund. This was done for a purpose.

"When Jesus had thus said, he was troubled in spirit, and testified, and said, Verily, verily, I say unto you, that one of you shall betray me. Then the disciples looked one on another, doubting of whom he spake. Now there was leaning on Jesus bosom one of his disciples, whom Jesus loved. Simon Peter therefore beckoned to him, that he should ask who it should be of whom he spake. He then lying on Jesus breast saith unto him, Lord, who is it? Jesus answered, He it is, to whom I shall give a sop, when I have dipped it. And when he had dipped the sop, he gave it to Judas Iscariot, the son of Simon. And after the sop Satan entered into him. Then said Jesus unto him, That thou doest , do quickly. Now no man at the table knew for what intent he spake this unto him. For some of them thought, because Judas had the bag, that Jesus had said unto him, Buy those things that we have need of against the feast; or, that he should give something to the poor." (**St John 13:21-30**)

To the other disciples it was perfectly acceptable for Judas to be absent from the group, as he was in charge of the money. They were quite used to him going out, for example, to buy supplies or to give to the poor. Some say that Judas was awarded this position of trust to enable him to reform and become a perfect disciple. Let us look at the events leading up to the great betrayal:

"Then one of the twelve, called Judas Iscariot, went unto the chief priests. And said unto them, What will ye give me, and I will deliver him unto you? And they covenanted with him for thirty pieces of silver. And from that time he sought opportunity to betray him." **(St Matthew 26:14-17)**

These chief priests, as with countless other people, knew exactly who Jesus was. There were many besides the disciples, therefore, who could have identified Jesus in order to secure his arrest.

Judas may have loved Jesus much more than the gospels tell us, maybe he was prepared to sacrifice himself to save his nation. From whichever direction he approached this Judas clearly wanted to be in first and use the situation to his own advantage, for the benefit of his cause. Being involved in the underground movement, he must have been privy to information regarding the authorities and the chief priests.

We are told that Judas negotiated with the chief priests and agreed to hand Jesus over to them for just thirty pieces of silver - symbolic of the traditional price paid for the weakest of slaves (as foretold in the scriptures by Zechariah).

The money was of secondary importance to Judas, despite his reputation. His main concern was to deliver the Jews; his aim to start a revolution and overthrow the Romans. The Jews had been promised, and were waiting for, the Messiah to release them. Judas would have been taught this as part of his upbringing. He was privileged to know that Jesus was, without doubt, the Messiah. He assumed therefore, that Jesus was the one who was going to set them free. He imagined physical liberation, i.e. by force - not spiritual liberation! Judas had to ask for money in order to strike a bargain with the chief priests; he was sure that if he were paid to deliver Jesus the plan would be followed up.

Judas now had to act quickly; he could not risk Jesus being maimed or killed - that would have undone all of his plans. He, like many others, believed himself to be in charge of this situation; Jesus was in fact always in control. Judas must have heard about an earlier meeting:

"Then assembled together the chief priests, and the scribes, and the elders of the people, unto the palace of the high priest, who was called Caiaphas. And consulted that they might take Jesus by subtilty, and kill him" **(St Matthew 26:3 -5)**

Judas came to the garden of Gethsemane and brought with him a cohort of Roman soldiers, together with guards sent by the chief priests and Pharisees, all carrying lanterns, torches and weapons. As far as Judas was concerned, the more guards and Roman soldiers the better - in fact he would have preferred the whole of the Roman army to have turned out. Judas believed that the time had come, that Jesus would resist arrest and would have no alternative but to release the power of his twelve legions of angels against them!

Judas had arranged a signal:

"And he that betrayed him had given them a token, saying, Whomsoever I shall kiss, that same is he: take him and lead him away safely." **(St Mark 14:44)**

Judas had to ensure that Jesus was well guarded for his plan to work. It was important that Jesus remained unharmed, fully aware and conscious. For Jesus and the disciples to be so outnumbered would provoke the rebellion Judas so longed for. He could not risk a surprise attack. By making such a condition, Judas believed that he was not leaving anything to chance and that he was giving Jesus the opportunity to call on the power! Judas never wanted for Jesus to be harmed; he certainly never expected for these events to lead to his death.

Judas stepped forward and amidst the flickering flames of innumerable torches and lanterns and the dancing shadows of the trees, appeared to kiss Jesus on the cheek.

The disciples had repeatedly fallen asleep and Jesus had scolded them for this:

"And he cometh, and findeth them sleeping, and saith unto Peter, Simon, sleepest thou? Couldest not thou watch one hour? Watch ye and pray, lest ye enter into temptation. The spirit truly is ready, but the flesh is weak. And again he went away, and prayed, and spake the same words. And when he returned, he found them

117

asleep again, (for their eyes were heavy,) neither wist they what to answer him. And he cometh the third time, and saith unto them, Sleep on now, and take your rest: it is enough, the hour is come; behold, the Son of man is betrayed into the hands of the sinners. Rise up, let us go; lo , he that betrayeth me is at hand." **(St Mark 14:37-43)**

Anyone who has slept out in the open air in such a climate will confirm that, after the day's glare of the sun, to fall asleep and then awaken to the cold night air, the eyes take a while to adjust to the surroundings. I therefore have to question the accounts of what the disciples saw. We have all been taught that Jesus was betrayed with a kiss, but St John (our eye witness) does not mention it! So did Judas kiss the cheek of his master - or did he simply whisper something in his ear?

Chapter 9
"IN GOD'S IMAGE"

The story of Adam and Eve, who were the 'kick-start' to the human race, is told in Genesis. God formed the first man, Adam, from the dust of the earth and placed him in the garden God had planted in Eden. As Adam slept, God took one of his ribs and closed up his flesh; from this rib God made a woman and brought her to Adam. They were both naked and as they did not realize this at this point, they felt no shame. The Garden of Eden, a paradise of birds, flowers, animals and trees, containing everything to fulfil their every need, was to be their home for eternity. In the middle of the garden were two special trees: the tree of life and the tree of knowledge of good and evil. God commanded Adam:

"... Of every tree of the garden thou mayest freely eat: But of the tree of the knowledge of good and evil, thou shalt not eat of it: for in the day that thou eatest thereof thou shalt surely die." **(Genesis 2:16-18)**

There is no description of the tree of knowledge recorded in the Bible; we can assume however, that it was a type of fruit tree. There is a description in *The Book of Enoch*:

"That tree is in height like the fir, and its leaves are like (those of) the Carob tree: and its fruit is like the clusters of the vine, very beautiful: and the fragrance of the tree penetrates afar. Then I said: How beautiful is the tree, and how attractive is its look! Then Raphael, the holy angel who was with me, answered me and said: 'This is the tree of wisdom, of which thy father old (in years) and thy aged mother, who were before thee, have eaten, and they learnt wisdom and their eyes were opened, and they knew that they were naked and they were driven out of the garden."

There is a description of the tree of life in the Bible, in the details of the spirit world given in the *Book of Revelation*:

"In the midst of the street of it, and on either side of the river, was there the tree of life, which bare twelve manner of fruits, and yielded her fruit every month: and the leaves of the tree were for the healing of the nations." **(Revelation 22:2)**

According to Genesis, Gods original plan was for Adam and

Eve and their descendants to live, for eternity, in this paradise on earth. They were the first children of God; as the Father, God wanted to share the joy of Creation with mankind. God created Adam and Eve to exist in the prime of life, never to grow any older; there was no ageing process as yet. Man had to have such a beginning in order for us to understand the true nature of God. Adam and Eve, devoid of emotion, were incapable of perception in terms of comprehending their situation, at this point. They suffered no hardship and had no need to think of future plans; the garden was to yield and provide all that they would ever require.

Adam was made from the soil and Eve from the rib of Adam; they were purely physical, earthly bodies, their spirits still dormant at this time. These bodies, designed to live forever did not, therefore, need to be dual-purpose.

"And God said, Let us make man in our image, after our likeness ..." **(Genesis 1:26)**

God says 'our image', i.e. uses the plural to emphasize that God is living, together with Jesus and others, in the spirit realms. Jesus says in a prayer to God:

"And now, O Father, glorify thou me with thine own self with the glory which I had with thee before the world was." **(St John 17:5)**

God and Jesus are in the spirit and so when God says, 'let us make man in our image', he is telling us that when man is created he will have a spirit.

"Then came to him certain of the Sadducees, which deny that there is any resurrection; and they asked him, saying, Master, Moses wrote unto us, If any man's brother die, having a wife, and he die without children, that his brother should take his wife, and raise up seed unto his brother. There were therefore seven brethren: and the first took a wife, and died without children. And the second took her to wife, and he died childless. And the third took her; and in like manner the seven also: and they left no children, and died. Last of all the woman died also. Therefore in the resurrection whose wife of them is she? for seven had her to wife. And Jesus answering said unto them. The children of this world marry, and are given in marriage: But they which shall be accounted worthy to obtain that

world, and the resurrection from the dead, neither marry, nor are given in marriage: Neither can they die any more: for the are equal unto the angels; and are the children of God, being the children of the resurrection. Now that the dead are raised, even Moses shewed at the bush, when he calleth the Lord the God of Abraham, and the God of Isaac, and the God of Jacob. For he is not a God of the dead, but of the living: for all live unto him." **(St Luke 20:27-39)**

The law at the time of Jesus was that if a man died, childless, his brother would marry his widow. The Sadducees, opposed to the Pharisees, did not believe in a spiritual resurrection of the dead. They asked this of Jesus, in a sarcastic manner, in the belief that they were posing a trick question. They thought at a very basic level, viewing the world in physical terms. Jesus has the opposite point of view and gives us a deeply spiritual answer. He takes the opportunity to teach, giving us an insight into the nature of existence in the spirit world. Jesus explains that marriage is a human concept and that on earth it is the man who has the authority and the power with such systems as arranged marriages and the giving and taking (of women) in marriage. He tells us that there is an afterlife and that in the spirit world we will 'live' forever as angels or spirits. Angels are neither male nor female, the woman now equal to the man; the domination and power of man over woman does not exist in the spirit world. We must assume, therefore, that Jesus is giving the message that the woman will not belong to any of her seven husbands. Just as in the spirit world, the spirit within the physical body on earth does not claim to be male or female.

This leads us to one of the great questions within the Christian Church - is God male or female? As God is spirit, God is asexual, neither male nor female. Traditionally, God has been identified as male - our prayers are to God the Father, etc. Most people regard God as male; in discussion with friends within the clergy, all at different stages of ordination, most told me that they could not worship or preach about an asexual God, that God for them was definitely male. All this has come from God's words:

"Let us make man in our image" **(Genesis 1:26)**

The first person created by God was Adam; Adam being a man and having been created in the image of God, the natural assumption has always been, therefore, that God is male. This theory has been handed down, from Old Testament times, through male-dominated laws, religion and society, through the writings of men for men.

Jesus gave us the Lord's Prayer, teaching us to address God as 'Our Father which art in heaven ...' Jesus refers to God as Father, he, him, etc., maintaining the Jewish tradition of the time which regarded God as male. If Jesus had contested or questioned this attitude in public his ministry would not have lasted for three years. He would not and could not change the language of the day in this matter. Later, after the Resurrection and Ascension, Jesus would reveal the truth to the disciples - only when in the spirit himself could he speak of this - and acknowledge the true nature of God as spirit and as such, neither male nor female.

The power to uphold the male domination we find throughout Jewish history has been drawn from the convenient story of Adam and Eve. From the very beginning of the creation of the human race, men have literally written their own authority over women. The Jews based the whole of their religion and society around sex discrimination. The ceremonial laws of the Jews, all for the benefit of men, treated women as second-class citizens. For me, the perfect example of men forging God's signature and designing laws for their own pleasure is found in Deuteronomy:

"When a man hath taken a wife, and married her, and it come to pass that she find no favour in his eyes, because he hath found some uncleanness in her: then let him write her a bill of divorcement, and give it in her hand, and send her out of his house. And when she is departed out of his house, she may go and be another man's wife. And if the latter husband hate her, and write her a bill of divorcement, and giveth it in her hand, and sendeth her out of his house, or if the latter husband die, which took her to be his wife; Her former husband, which sent her away, may not take her again to be his wife, after that she is defiled; for that is abomination before the Lord: and thou shalt not cause the land to sin, which the Lord they God giveth thee for an inheritance." **(Deuteronomy 24:1-5)**

Jesus talks about this in the gospels:

"It hath been said, Whosoever shall put away his wife, let

122

him give her a writing of divorcement: But I say unto you, That whosoever shall put away his wife, saving for the cause of fornication, causeth her to commit adultery: and whosoever shall marry her that is divorced committeth adultery." (**St Matthew 5:31-3**)

Jesus is telling the people that this law has been abused and although they believe that they are acting within the law, it is actually turning them into adulterers. The men had all the rights; a woman could not instigate a divorce. Men were using this law for themselves as an excuse to change wives and presenting these writs for the wrong, probably trivial, reasons. Here Jesus, the socialist, feminist, egalitarian, sheds fresh light on this old man-made law. Jesus says:

"Think not that I am come to destroy the law, or the prophets: I am not come to destroy, but to fulfil." (**St Matthew 5:17**)

Churches are now reluctantly ordaining women as priests, claiming to be 'moving with the times'. The time has always been right - what has been wrong is the superficial way in which sin and shame have been placed at the feet of Eve. Let us continue to explore Adam and Eve in the garden of Eden and, in doing so, I hope to rescue Eve and turn the tables on men:

"Now the serpent was more subtil than any beast of the field which the Lord God had made. And he said unto the woman, Yea, hath God said, Ye shall not eat of every tree of the garden: And the woman said unto the serpent, We may eat of the fruit of the trees of the garden: But of the fruit of the tree which is in the midst of the garden, God hath said, Ye shall not eat of it, neither shall ye touch it, lest ye die. And the serpent said unto the woman, Ye shall not surely die: For God doth know that in the day ye eat thereof, then your eyes shall be opened, and ye shall be as gods, knowing good and evil. And when the woman saw that the tree was good for food, and that it was pleasant to the eyes, and a tree to be desired to make one wise, she took of the fruit thereof, and did eat, and gave also unto her husband with her; and he did eat. And the eyes of them both were opened, and they knew that they were naked; and they sewed fig leaves together, and made themselves aprons." (**Genesis 3:1-8**)

The serpent represents the negative, evil aspect of the physical side of man. God placed Adam and Eve in a perfect paradise, their survival guaranteed, without the need for the knowledge of good and evil. This knowledge, their emotions and spirits dormant within them, they were not able to recognise at this time. Without this experience Eve was, therefore, not able to comprehend the treachery of the serpent. Eating the fruit was to activate this knowledge, was to awaken their emotions and spirits (within), giving them the intelligence to think for themselves. The spirit ignited, Adam and Eve would become spiritual as well as physical. Just as the buds of spring burst into flower, the explosion within would give birth to a brand new spirit, creating the dual-purpose body. Suddenly, acutely aware and sensitive, their eyes would be opened and they would see the transformation in each other, see the outward image of the spirit - the aura.

From this we can understand the true nature of God. Adam and Eve disobeyed God and ate the fruit from the tree; it was, therefore, the physical side of man that let God down. Even though God later expelled Adam and Eve from the garden for this, God's intention was not to abandon them. God's plan is that only physical nature will be lost. As soon as Adam and Eve ate the fruit they started to die - the ageing process had been set in motion. Mankind now has a time limit on earthly life.

"In the sweat of thy face shalt thou eat bread, till thou return unto the ground; for out of it wast thou taken: for dust thou art, and unto dust shalt thou return" (**Genesis 3:19**)

Here, God reassures us all that it is only the physical body that will now return to the soil at death. To ensure that all is not lost God will take back that which belongs to God. Before a Committal, the minister may say:

"I heard a voice from heaven, saying, Write this: 'Happy are the dead who die in the faith of Christ! Henceforth', says the Spirit, 'they may rest from their labours; for they take with them the record of their deeds.'" (**Revelation 14:13**)

Here an angel explains to St John that a dead body does not need a record of its earthly life; this body will in time decay in the ground and become dust. The record of deeds accompanies the spirit body and will determine its place within the 'many mansions'.

Eating the fruit of the tree of knowledge of good and evil was the first sin against God; it was the first time that anyone had 'missed the mark'. This would not have featured in their records as Adam and Eve were not yet spiritually awakened. The record of deeds, attached to the spirit body would not have included what happened in the garden of Eden. God banished Adam and Eve from the garden and the sin was forgotten. It is man who insists on perpetuating the attitude that only Eve acted against God's will. Eve has been made the scapegoat in order to award the power to men within the male-dominated religions of this world.

It was only after Adam and Eve had been expelled from the garden that they understood what the garden represented. As God's children they had been privileged to enjoy paradise on earth; only after eating the fruit were they capable of realising this.

The ideal of the Garden of Eden is common to many world religions. There are many who cannot understand the spiritual side of life or what happens to us at death. In order to merge the spiritual and physical sides of life man has therefore created the idea of a regained earthly paradise. Those who are willing to conform to a particular religion, and way of life, are promised this inheritance as their reward; they are taught that they could earn their right to a place in a comfortable earthly paradise.

To God, Adam and Eve were equally guilty; God did not blame Eve alone. We can see this in the way God's punishment is evenly balanced. By eating the fruit, Eve was awarded the sorrow of her reproductive system. Adam now had to work hard on the land, plant and harvest, to provide food to ensure their survival. It is man who has tilted the scales, continually regarding Eve to be at fault, conveniently overlooking some very important points. It was Adam who was given the direct command from God not to eat from the tree of knowledge of good and evil; he would have passed this information to Eve. Yet he stood back as the serpent deceived her. The serpent addressed Eve only, Adam did not defend her or remind her of God's commandment. Adam offered no resistance and remained silent - hardly the behaviour representative of the head of the household! Adam in fact, allowed Eve to dominate him!

The serpent's part in this was to make sure that Adam and Eve defied the command from God, which Eve had repeated. Eating the fruit was to completely alter their state of being. They became fully human, with the five physical senses, plus spiritual senses; with this, most importantly, came the ability to reproduce.

God had created the perfect situation and it was Adam and Eve, not God, who altered it. Adam and Eve were not yet aware of right and wrong; it was through their naivety and weakness, that they disobeyed God. As a result of this, they were never to be allowed back into the garden - they may have been tempted to eat from the tree of knowledge again or even from the tree of life! This was man's first great lesson: go against God and you must face the consequences. God does not turn back! God had to prevent Adam and Eve from embracing the antidote to the serpent's sting - the tree of life! They were not going to be given this second chance of paradise on earth; God would not allow this:

"And the Lord God said, Behold, the man is become as one of us, to know good and evil: and now, lest he put forth his hand, and take also of the tree of life, and eat, and live for ever: Therefore the Lord God sent him forth from the garden of Eden, to till the ground from whence he was taken. So he drove out the man; and he placed at the east of the garden of Eden Cherubims, and a flaming sword which turned every way, to keep the way of the tree of life." **(Genesis 3:22-4)**

The garden of Eden was replaced by a fully-human existence. Adam and Eve had gained the wisdom and knowledge to live outside of the garden. They had lost paradise but gained worldly knowledge. The spirit now gave them the choice to learn right from wrong. From now on they would progress towards spiritual eternity and the serpent knew this!

In the heavenly Jerusalem the tree of life represents eternal life, within the spirit world. In the garden of Eden, the tree of life represents physical eternal life - paradise on earth.

How long did Adam and Eve live in the garden of Eden? The Bible gives us no indication of the time period between their creation and eating the fruit from the tree of knowledge. In my opinion, they must have spent a considerable amount of time experiencing their paradise garden. Whatever the time period involved there was never any question of Adam and Eve producing children, whilst living in the garden of Eden. It was when they ate of the fruit that not only

126

their senses, but also the concept of time, were born. It is recorded in the Bible that they produced children outside of the garden. In order for the human race to begin, Adam and Eve had to become fully human themselves and that existence had to be outside of the garden. Living in the garden, they were not yet fully human and therefore incapable of reproduction.

If Adam and Eve had produced children in the garden of Eden, they would have been the perfect offspring of perfect parents. This would not have served the purpose, would not have brought man to know God. For Old Testament religion this first lesson had to come straight away - the first example of 'sin' had to come from the very first couple! Out of the garden, the 'sins of the fathers' were transferred to Cain and Abel and the worst sin: "man's inhumanity to man" was born; Cain murdered his brother, Abel.

The serpent says:

"... in the day ye eat thereof, then your eyes shall be opened, and ye shall be as gods, knowing good and evil." **(Genesis 3:5)**

This is exactly what happened. Adam and Eve ate of the fruit and their 'spiritual' eyes were opened; they now realised that they were naked. They saw not only their physical bodies, but also the spiritual aura. They could read each other's thoughts and lust was born into the harmony of creation. In the many mansions all spirits see each other's naked form; sexual arousal does not prevail - only eternal love!

"And they heard the voice of the Lord God walking in the garden in the cool of the day: and Adam and his wife hid themselves from the presence of the Lord God amongst the trees of the garden. And the Lord God called unto Adam, and said unto him, Where art thou? And he said, I heard they voice in the garden, and I was afraid, because I was naked; and I hid myself; And he said, Who told thee that thou wast naked? Hast thou eaten of the tree, whereof I commanded thee that thou shouldest not eat?" **(Genesis 3:8-12)**

Many theologians and biblical scholars have written on this subject, through the ages, using Eve as the scapegoat. They point the finger at Eve in order to give men authority and the right to dominate women. Here I cannot resist a quote (about Eve) from Tertullian (c160-c220), a Carthaginian theologian, known as the father of Latin theology, who was the creator of ecclesiastical Latiny:

"You are the Devil's gateway. You are the unsealer of that forbidden tree. You are the first deserter of the divine law. You are she who persuaded him whom the Devil was not valiant enough to attack. You destroyed so easily God's image man. On account of your desert, that is death, even the Son of God had to die."

Adam's punishment was to till the ground, which would now yield not just brambles, but also thistles and the future of man became dependent on the seasons of nature. Along with the human attributes gained by eating the fruit, came the seasons of man.

Let me now share with you my interpretation of the four seasons of man:

Let us first rest our minds in the affirmation that death is as normal as birth, and as such within God's plan.

We all experience seasons in our lives. According to the Bible, we are supposed to have a life-span of three score and ten years. If we split this time into four seasons, in the same way as in nature, we experience spring, summer, autumn and winter in our physical lives. In these modern times, people are living on average much longer; I will use for illustration, therefore, approximately twenty years for each season.

From birth until our early twenties, is the springtime - the first quarter of our lives. From this time until our early forties, is the summertime - the second quarter. From this time until our early sixties becomes the autumn, the third quarter. From this time until we pass out of this life is the winter and the last quarter spent in our physical bodies.

Our physical bodies, in the springtime of our lives as in nature, require all the ingredients for solid growth - both physically and spiritually. Our senses, mind and physical shape develop to carry us into the next phase of life. This first phase forms the foundation of our lives - who we are and what we may be capable of achieving throughout the following three phases of our lives. Some people might be late developers, but usually a child will have a particular interest or passion and will develop this throughout life. Sometimes a child will reveal a sudden spark of talent and then it will disappear;

later in life, parents will recall that memory when the child recaptures that talent or gift. In the animal world the same thing occurs; many a famous racehorse, greyhound or other 'performing' animal will show its class during early training. It is often only the eye of an expert, in that particular field of study, that will see this early talent or gift and sure enough the spotter will see the flower blossom during their lifetime.

Come the summertime we are now in full bloom, as mature adults. For most, however, this is not a gentle transition and is often a jolt into the reality of the physical world. There are many reasons for this, the most obvious being choosing a partner, parenthood and earning a living in a chosen career, after years of study. What was once a single mind, within a single body, takes on the plural and the majority become responsible for partners and children, and to employers. As the pond grows larger more ripples float out from within. We may experience financial hardship as our extra responsibilities have to fit within a fixed working wage. We buy or rent a home, which we also have to maintain. We need transport to travel back and forth, for our employment and family recreation. During this particular phase of our physical lives, we begin to lose that polished edge. As children grow to teenagers, routine has become the name of the game and any diversion may upset what has had to be a stable few years. We have now had the experience or feeling pain when loved ones have been ill or upset. Many people experience marriage breakdowns and children become divided between parents. It is in this portion of life that we feel, for the first time, the wind blowing against our faces.

Summertime blends into autumn, the third phase; we are now in our early forties and most have experienced half of their life span in the physical body. Already our children have started to tread the path of life's journey; according to their stage of life, we can look both backwards, to remember where we once were, and forwards, to refocus future plans. We are now able to understand where our parents once were and that we have come half-way through life.

The physical body begins to change, skin and bone begin to act differently, hair colour changes and hair loss becomes apparent. We begin to wonder about the things that we might have done earlier in our lives. Some call this the mid-life crisis. We now start to look forward into life again. We may try to fulfil some of our dreams or ambitions and finally get around to projects we feel that we missed out on. At the same time we may be thinking of 'putting a little by' to prepare for the last phase of physical life.

By the autumn years, many will have come across some kind of religion, either through crisis, baptism, wedding or funeral. We all have different experiences of this. No matter how we deal with the subject of religion it crops up in daily life, as if to remind us that if we have not tested it yet, perhaps we should. We are at that in-between stage and may think that we have experienced all the trials and tribulations of everyday life, and enjoyed all possible festivities; we may have travelled the globe, have the security of a healthy bank balance, and the children may be 'off our hands' and doing well, etc. We may feel that life has been good so far or we may feel that we have had a raw deal. Why do we need religion for either case? Many feel that there is something missing, something else, something more in life. In order to account for their lot in life, many look beyond for reasons and answers. We look for God in the Church, Mosque or Synagogue. Which building does God visit the most? God does not live in any of these buildings! God lives inside men and women and in order to stop this panic, this is the best place to look for him.

This autumn phase can also be one of the most enjoyable times - as we are hopefully beginning to 'level out' our lives. Wisdom is starting to show itself and not always, we may think, for our own good. An overactive mind does not always compensate for an ageing physical body; wisdom may become the replacement for the weary. Grandparenthood is the compensation for many who feel that they may have lost out on some earlier joy, caught up in the turmoil of brining up their own children. Most of all, grandparents see that physical looks, more often than not, skip a generation, and so the grandchildren become a reflection of their former selves. Grandparents look at their children, rearing their grandchildren, and in so doing recall a time where they once were. The great prophet, Isaiah, said that in order to see the future look into the past.

We have travelled along life's highway and reached the final season in life. As surely and as silently as the moon appears in the sky, so comes the winter season of our lives. We gently blend from autumn to winter just as day blends into night and we arrive, without any fuss, in our sixties. Pain is brought about by the ageing process and the wear and tear on the physical body, caused by past toil. For many, it is a winter of discontent, the obvious reasons for this being retirement and ill-health. Wisdom hair is abundant and the frame of the body has lost its elasticity; a mere cut or bruise takes longer to heal. Sometimes the mind wanders and the gaze could have the innocence of a young child or the wisdom of one with knowledge of life and nature; all the joy and splendour of many years twinkles in the pupil like a distant star in the calm night sky.

It is at this stage that the family network should kick into action. Charity first begins at home and now is our chance to receive the love, care and support we gave to our children. This can only be a means to an end and part of God's plan for us all. We have now come full circle and the answer to man's destiny is in the hands of the Creator.

With the circle complete, if this evidence is accepted, it makes death a mere milestone, not the end of a journey. The physical body is returned to the ground and the spirit body begins a brand-new dawn within the 'many mansions' on a journey of progression, towards the centre of our rainbow wheel.

For as St Paul wrote to Timothy:

"For this is good and acceptable in the sight of God our Saviour; Who will have all men to be saved, and to come unto the knowledge of the truth." **(Timothy 2:3-5)**

In this we have the highest authority for believing that the great shepherd himself will not be content if even one of his sheep is missing from the fold.

In *Revelation*, we have a description of the heavenly Jerusalem, which includes a description of the tree of life:

"In the midst of the street of it, and on either side of the river, was there the tree of life, which bare twelve manner of fruits, and yielded her fruit every month: and the leaves of the tree were for the healing of the nations" **(Revelation 22:2)**

For me, this tree symbolises Eve, the mother of mankind.

131

God gave life to Eve and as she was the source of all human life, from this we attain the beginning of the human race. Herein lies the triumph of Eve! Whether history, myth or legend - Eve is our heroine!

The tree of life, within the very heart of the rainbow mansions, can only be compared to the story of Eve. Eve is the family tree; she ate of the fruit and in becoming human, became fruitful herself. Menstruation began and she conceived Cain and Abel. From her therefore, came the twelve tribes of Israel; Eve is responsible for the differing ethnic groups of man.

"The sum of generations is therefore: fourteen from Abraham to David; fourteen from David to the Babylonian deportation; and fourteen from the Babylonian deportation to Christ" (**Matthew 1:17**)

We have now come full circle. The first Adam is to be found in Genesis, in the Old Testament. He was created, by God, from the soil. We find the second Adam, Jesus Christ, in the New Testament. He was created by God to prove the spiritual resurrection. St Paul tells us:

"And so it is written, The first man Adam was made a living soul; the last Adam was made a quickening spirit. Howbeit that was not first which is spiritual, but that which is natural; and afterwards that which is spiritual. The first man is of the earth, earthly: the second man is the Lord from heaven. As is the earthy, such are they also that are earthy: and as is the heavenly, such are they also that are heavenly. And as we have borne the image of the earthy, we shall also bear the image of the heavenly." (**1 Corinthians 15:45-50**)

These two Adams, created as complete opposites, bring togther the Old and New Testaments. St Paul helps us to understand this:

"For since by man came death, by man came also the resurrection of the dead. For as in Adam all die, even so in Christ shall all be made alive. But every man in his own order: Christ the firstfruits; afterward they that are Christ's at his coming." (**1 Corinthians 15:21-4**)

Here, St Paul shows us a perfect example of the contrast between the first and second Adams. Through the first Adam, death -

the end of physical life on earth - was introduced. Christ, the second Adam, *"the firstfruits of them that slept"* (**1 Corinthians 15:20**), was the first to make the transition directly back to God in the heavenly Jerusalem, at the heart of the rainbow mansions. Christ came to prove that we all have eternal life. Our transition is a journey of progression towards that heavenly Jerusalem. Jesus Christ is the perfect fulfilment of the ideal of Adam and it is his exultation that reverses the fall of Adam. St Paul refers to 'Christ the firstfruits; afterward they that are Christ's at his coming'; Christ now glorified at the centre of the rainbow mansions, 'his coming' indicating the glorious second coming, will take his victory ride opening the seven seals at the end of life on earth:

"And I heard a great voice out of heaven saying, Behold, the tabernacle of God is with men, and he will dwell with them, and they shall be his people, and God himself shall be with them, and be their God." (**Revelation 21:3**)

Eve was the first woman on earth, the mother of mankind, made the scapegoat of her own people and Christians through the ages. To look at the genealogy of Eve, we have only the rib of Adam. Made from his rib, Eve was the descendant of Adam and Adam her only ancestor. She must, therefore, have been created with the DNA of Adam. Eve was created as an associate and equal for Adam; she was not therefore a second class citizen.

"And the Lord God said, It is not good that the man should be alone; I will make him an help meet for him." (**Genesis 2:18**)

"And Adam said, This is now bone of my bones, and flesh of my flesh: she shall be called Woman, because she was taken out of Man." (**Genesis 2:23**)

In the garden of Eden, God said to the serpent:

"And I will put enmity between thee and the woman, and between thy seed and her seed; it shall bruise thy head, and thou shalt bruise his heel." (**Genesis 3:15**)

God is telling the serpent, who represents they physical nature of man, that this 'corruptible' (i.e. the physical side of man) will be overcome by the introduction of the 'incorruptible', in the form of one of Eve's descendants. This, of course, is the first reference in the Bible to Christ, who will be victorious over the serpent's descendants; not ascribing this victory to Eve's descendants in general, but to one of her future sons. A wonderful golden thread runs through the Bible from within the garden of Eden to the birth of Jesus Christ and is the fulfilment of what God had said.

I am now going to share with you some of the great teachings from the gospels of St Matthew and St Luke, who have given us the genealogy of Jesus. St Matthew reveals the genealogy of Joseph and St Luke reveals the genealogy of Mary. I find these fascinating as they contain the whole of the history of God's chosen people, the sovereignty of God and all the weakness of mankind. These two genealogies are the fulfilment of all that the prophets foretold.

Let us first look at St Matthew, Chapter 1, as he gives us his version of the genealogy of Jesus Christ, son of David, beginning with Abraham, through fourteen generations to King David. The prophets predicted the coming of the Messiah, that he would descend, through the princely line, from David and that he would be born in Bethlehem:

"And they said unto him, In Bethlehem of Judea: for thus it is written by the prophet. And thou Bethlehem, in the land of Juda, are not the least among the princes of Juda: for out of thee shall come a Governor, that shall rule my people Israel." **(St Matthew 2:5-7)**

This is referring to the prophecy (of Micah) made some seven hundred years before the birth of Christ.

King David fathered Solomon (his mother had been the wife of Uriah) and it is through this son of David that we find the genealogy of Joseph. Matthew takes us through another fourteen generations of kings, until we reach the Babylonian deportation, which brings us within six hundred years of the birth of Christ. God now put a curse on this line of the kings of Judah, as the prophet Jeremiah tells us:

"As I live, saith the Lord, though Coniah the son of Jehoiakim King of Judah were the signet upon my right hand, yet would I pluck thee thence; And I will give thee into the hand of them that seek thy life, and into the hand of them whose face thou fearest, even into the hand of Nebuchadrezzar King of Babylon, and into the

hand of the Chaldeans. And I will cast thee out, and thy mother that bare thee, into another country, where ye were not born; and there shall ye die. But to the land whereunto they desire to return, thither shall they not return." **(Jeremiah 22:24-28)**

"Thus saith the Lord, Write ye this man childless, a man that shall not prosper in his days: for no man of his seed shall prosper, sitting upon the throne of David, and ruling any more in Judah." **(Jeremiah 22:30)**

Indeed, that was the end of the reign of kings through the line of David, for the time being, and no-one sat on the throne of David for the next six hundred years. Joseph was a descendant of this curse; if Christ, therefore, had been the son of Joseph, he could not have reigned on the throne of David through this line. However, Zerubbabel, grandson of Jechonias (Coniah) did manage to become governor, not king, of Judah on his return from exile.

Another fourteen generations later, following the Babylonian deportation, we finally reach Joseph:

"And Jacob begat Joseph the husband of Mary, of whom was born Jesus, who is called Christ". **(Matthew 1:16)**

The genealogy up to this point speaks only of the male line, using the term 'begat'; each man begat (fathered) his son. This suddenly stops at Joseph; Jesus was born of Mary. This genealogy spans two thousand years, from Abraham to Jesus; the six hundred year old curse must dispute Joseph as the biological father of Jesus, making him just an adoptive parent. On this evidence, Joseph could not possibly have been the father of Jesus.

Let us now look at St Luke 3:23 onwards for the genealogy of Mary, which traces this pure line back to Adam, head of the human race. This proves Jesus to be a direct descendant of Adam and connects the first and second Adams, bringing Adam of the Old Testament through to Jesus of the New Testament. By tracing this particular genealogy from Adam to Jesus, this gospel writer highlights the fact, linking the first and second Adams, that neither had been conceived through a human father. This genealogy of Mary comes not through David's son, Solomon, but through another son, Nathan, whose line was curse-free. Through this royal line, which had to be pure, was born of Mary the son of God, Jesus Christ.

"And in the sixth month the angel Gabriel was sent from God unto a city of Galilee, named Nazareth. To a virgin espoused to a man whose name was Joseph, of the house of David; and the virgin's name was Mary. And the angel came in unto her, and said, Hail, thou art highly favoured, the Lord is with thee: blessed art thou among women. And when she saw him she was troubled at his saying, and cast in her mind what manner of salutation this should be. And the angel said unto her, Fear not, Mary: for thou hast found favour with God. And, behold, thou shalt conceive in thy womb, and bring forth a son , and shalt call his name JESUS. He shall be great, and shall be called the Son of the Highest: and the Lord God shall give unto him the throne of this father David: And he shall reign over the house of Jacob for ever; and of his kingdom there shall be no end." **(St Luke 1:26-34)**

THE END